A Legacy of
Sephardic,
Mediterranean,
and American Recipes

RACHEL ALMELEH

LifeRich Publishing is a registered trademark of The Reader's Digest Association, Inc.

LifeRich Publishing books may be ordered through booksellers or by contacting:

LifeRich Publishing
1663 Liberty Drive
Bloomington, IN 47403
www.liferichpublishing.com
1 (888) 238-8637

Because of the dynamic nature of the Internet, any web addresses or links contained in this book may have changed since publication and may no longer be valid. The views expressed in this work are solely those of the author and do not necessarily reflect the views of the publisher, and the publisher hereby disclaims any responsibility for them.

Any people depicted in stock imagery provided by Thinkstock are models, and such images are being used for illustrative purposes only. Certain stock imagery © Thinkstock.

ISBN: 978-1-4897-0345-3 (sc)
ISBN: 978-1-4897-0346-0 (e)

Library of Congress Control Number: 2014921761

Printed in the United States of America.

LifeRich Publishing rev. date: 12/30/2014

Contents

INTRODUCTION: MY STORY

Where to begin? I am not writing this book to make money, but because cooking Sephardic food is my passion. According to Tarot.com my mission in life is to nurture. My daughter broke out laughing when I told her that, but I believe it's true. One of the ways I nurture is to share food, especially Sephardic food.

Both of my parents, Jacob D. Almeleh and Emily Capelouto were Sephardic, born on the Isle of Rhodes. For those not familiar with this ethnicity, Sephardic refers mainly to Jews who were expelled from Spain during the Inquisition of 1492, many of which were allowed to settle in the Ottoman Empire. Rhodes was Turkish and then became Greek and then Italian and is now Greek again. My parents attended a French Jewish parochial school called The Alliance Israelite. No wonder my father spoke seven languages! Both of my parents immigrated to Seattle at different times as Italians. They met and married in the U.S. My mother never spoke English well and only became a US citizen just three years before she died at age 48. My father tutored her as he did for many other immigrants. Dad always spoke to my sister and me in English. He would say, "When in Rome, do as the Romans do."

So, you can imagine the Mediterranean influences in Sephardic cooking and even in the Spanish language which incorporated many words of other languages, especially when the original word was forgotten. Being that I taught modern Spanish for 25 years, I also noticed the grammatical and pronunciation differences. The language became known as Ladino or Judezmo. The names of many recipes are in Ladino. Mediterranean ingredients include many vegetables, olive oil, fish and tomato sauce.

Unfortunately, my mother became very ill after I was born, in and out of hospitals, and died when I was twelve and my sister, Esther, fourteen. The good news: "Mommy", as I always called her, was a good cook and very economical, always finding a way to use food before it went bad. Have sour milk? Make yogurt! Got spoiling fruit my Dad brought home from the Pike Place Market where he worked? Make compote, jam. The bad news: my sister and I did not get to watch and learn how to make Sephardic food. We had a nanny when Mom was in the hospital or bedridden. We were not wealthy in money, but I never considered myself poor. I never went hungry!

After my mother passed, my sister and I took on the responsibility of cooking dinner for Dad and us. "Adio, Señor del Mundo"! (G-d, King of the Universe!) First attempt at Spanish rice: burned! Second attempt at Spanish rice: mush! No matter how it turned out, our Dad ate it! "Paciencia, que mos manda el Dio"! (G-d, give us patience!)

We spent many holidays with aunts and uncles on both sides of the family. Good Sephardic traditions! But I wanted the food more often. I started visiting my aunties to watch them cook and I would take notes. I watched my Auntie Rae (Capelouto) make her own fillo dough stretching it out over the covered kitchen table and putting all kinds of fillings in it. I watched my Auntie Matty (Greenberg) make boyos, stretching the dough on an oiled plate and sprinkling cheese on it before filling with spinach. I also helped her make biscochos. She always claimed hers were better than Auntie Rae's. I watched Auntie Glavina (Almeleh) make masa de vino and potato burmuelos for Passover. I was not interested, however, in her mioyo (fried calves' brains). And I learned how to make pepitada and suplach for breaking the fast on Yom Kippur from my petite Auntie Victoria (Almeleh). Over the years I have continued to learn secrets and tips from many cousins. I received my first Sephardic cookbook as a wedding gift from my cousin Mary Halela.

Reading recipes without the little secret tips will not always guarantee success. I practiced on burecas the most. My cousin Vivian Greenberg thought we should try to sell them to the airlines as snacks. Better than peanuts! Alas, life got busy with two children and a teaching career. As my marriage was falling apart and I had to become my father's guardian after his stroke, I fell apart and wound up divorcing. I no longer felt hindered to start a business selling Sephardic food. Enter Rachel's Sephardic Delicacies, a one-woman home-based hobby business! I started from an apartment in Federal Way, Washington.

Why sell the food? Just as I got busy with life, so do many others. A lot of the yummiest Sephardic comfort food is time consuming and sometimes tricky to make. I was working part-time and had summers off when I started. In the baby boomer generation many women worked. And as the older generation no longer had the stamina and ability to cook these foods, I could make the food and deliver it right to their door!

This book documents my labor of love and provides a legacy of traditions for my family and others. There are a lot of non-Sephardic favorite recipes, too. There are lots of tips from my experience and experimenting with modern day concerns for nut allergies, gluten-free and vegetarian preferences plus a healthy Mediterranean diet.

Come con gana! (Eat with pleasure!)

Rachel Almeleh

Teaching my grandson, Jacob, to make burecas in 2006

SAVORY PASTRIES

A meal or an appetizer

OH BOY! BOYOS! BULEMAS de SPINACA! (Individual Spinach Pastries)

Boyos are often referred to as "dezayuno", which means breakfast in Ladino, because it is a breakfast favorite served with hard-boiled eggs and sometimes yogurt.

Notes: Best results are with fresh Spinach. To save time, you can buy triple-washed spinach, but it will cost more because it is usually baby spinach. Otherwise, wash the spinach and let dry on the counter overnight. Give yourself a few hours. I often chop the spinach the night before. Or chop spinach while dough is rising. Make sure it is dry. Get help to make it go faster. My sister, Esther, of blessed memory, used to help me. She said: "I'm the roller, you're the filler." You can increase or decrease the recipe. The difference between a boyo and a bulema is the shape. A boyo is square or oblong and a bulema is a round coil. Yum! As my sister would say, "Better than sex"! Bulemas were originally made with homemade fillo stretched paper-thin over a table as I watched my Auntie Rae Capelouto do.

Recipe for about 20 bulemas or 30 boyos.

Dough
1 tsp. yeast
2 cups lukewarm water
6-7 cups flour
Pinch of salt
2 tbsp. oil
Oil to cover pan ¼" for letting dough stand

Dissolve yeast in 1/2 cup of the lukewarm water until it bubbles, about 10 minutes. Pour 6 cups flour into large bowl (I use an electric mixer bowl with a knead attachment). Add yeast, salt and oil. Rub through. Start adding rest of water slowly. Add more flour as needed and knead by hand or machine. By hand, pull apart and re-knead until dough is smooth and shiny.

Pour 1/4 inch of oil into the bottom of an oblong pan. Divide dough into balls, slightly flattened. Dip both sides in oil and place in pan covered tightly with plastic wrap to rest for about 20 minutes.

After filling, place boyos on a greased baking sheet about 1-2 inches apart. Brush with beaten egg and sprinkle with cheese. **Bake in preheated oven at 400° for 25-30 minutes.** Practice! Practice!

Filling

2 ½ lbs. fresh spinach, washed or 2 pre-washed cartons
1/4 cup flour for dusting
1 ½-2 cups Parmesan or Romano cheese to taste
½ -1 cup crumbled feta to taste

Topping

1 beaten egg
Parmesan cheese

Chop cleaned spinach, but not too fine or it will become too wet and lose vitamins. Use a large bowl. Dust spinach with flour to take up residual moisture. Add the cheeses and mix. Next, spray your baking pans with oil or layer parchment paper. Oil or spray the surface for rolling out the dough.

RECTANGULAR OR CIGAR SHAPE

Take a ball of dough and roll it about 8" by 6" wide and stretch it out by hand if you want it thinner. (I just use the rolling pin.) Take a handful of filling to make a boyo. (I use large tongs to grab spinach) Place it at bottom of your rectangle and fold over the outer ends about an inch or two and start rolling or flipping the dough over tightly squeezed-in spinach. You might get a semi-flat or large cigar shape. Make sure there are no holes in dough or any spinach leaking out. If you get a small hole on top, egg and cheese topping can fill it in.

Bake at 400⁰ for 25-30 minutes.

SMALL SQUARE SHAPE

Divide dough ball into 2. Roll out a circle about 6 inches in diameter. Put filling in center and fold in the sides.

COIL SHAPE

For a coiled bulema, stretch dough into an 8-10 inch rectangle or square. Fill lengthwise at one end. Fold in edges and roll tightly being careful not to create holes. Roll into a coil, tucking one end under the coil.

BULEMAS

FILLING A BULEMA

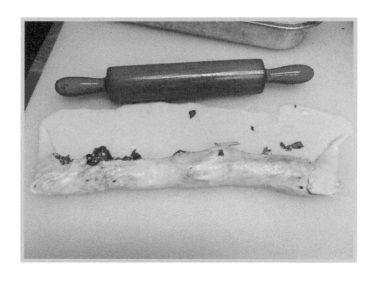

ROLLING A BULEMA

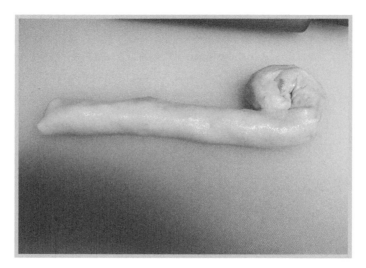

COILING A BULEMA

BULEMAS ON A PAN

BOYOS

FILLING A BOYO

ROLLING A BOYO

BOYOS AND BULEMAS ON A PLATE

Note: You can freeze them in plastic bags when thoroughly cooled. If you have time and space, freeze boyos in one layer on a baking sheet before placing in a bag

<u>Gluten-free:</u> Use Namaste or other brand all-purpose gluten-free flour. Reduce yeast by ¼ tsp., increase flour by 2 tbsp. and salt by ¼ tsp.

Potato Filling

3-4 lbs. potatoes, mashed
1-1 ½ cups Parmesan cheese
½ cup feta (some add 1 cup cottage cheese)
3-4 eggs
1 tsp. salt

Eggplant Filling

1 large eggplant, peeled and cubed
1 onion, chopped
½ cup drained canned tomatoes
3 tbsp. oil
½ cup potato flakes
1 tsp. salt
½ cup grated Parmesan cheese
¼ cup feta cheese
¼ tsp. sugar

Soak eggplant in salted water. Drain and squeeze out moisture. Sauté the onion. Add eggplant, tomatoes and salt. Simmer about 30 minutes. When cool, add egg, cheese, potato flakes and sugar.

BURECAS

(Baked turnovers with varied vegetable or rice fillings)

Recipe for 40-50 burecas.
<u>Dough</u>:
1 cup vegetable oil
2 ½ cups water
1 tsp. salt
6-7 cups white flour
Bring the oil, water, and salt to a boil. Remove the pan from the heat. Stir in 6 cups of flour quickly. Add more flour so dough feels like pie dough. Knead it until smooth. Transfer to a bowl and cover to prevent drying out. I just use a pan cover. You can use wax paper.

The traditional hand method of making the turnovers is time-consuming and takes a lot of practice. I prefer to use a tool. Both methods are here explained.

<u>Hand Method</u>: Divide dough into walnut-sized balls. Keep them covered. Roll out each into a circular shape 3- 4 inches in diameter. Place about a tablespoon of desired filling in the middle. (see below for filling recipes) Fold over the dough and press edges together by either fluting them or pressing with the tines of a fork.

<u>Tools:</u>

1. You can use the rim of a can or glass to uniformly cut turnover edges.
2. You can use a round cookie cutter.

3. I use a plastic dough press that can be purchased on-line or in a kitchen store like Sur la Table. Unfortunately, you might have to buy a set of different sizes. I use the different sizes to make pasteles (meat pies) and party-size appetizers.

Roll out a large amount of dough about ¼ "and then cut out several dough circles with the press. Place a circle on top of the press, put in the filling and push together tightly while holding the filled side to avoid cracks. The press has a design edge. Push in filling side and open the press to extract a perfect and uniform turnover. Re-use the dough from cutting with more dough from the bowl. Put burecas on an oiled (I use spray) baking pan or line tray with parchment paper.

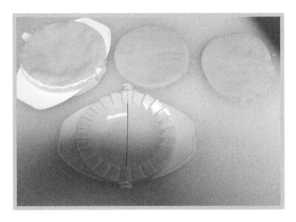

DOUGH PRESS TOOL

BURECAS

MY GRANDSON, JACOB, RELISHING A BURECA WITH HIS FATHER, VICTOR CARLBOM

Topping: Beat an egg and brush the tops. Sprinkle to taste with grated Parmesan cheese. If you are watching calories, use light Parmesan. Bake in a preheated oven at 400⁰ for 25-30 minutes or until light brown.

Cool and store burecas in plastic bags or containers. They can be frozen and reheated. Reheat from frozen in a 250⁰ oven for 10-15 minutes or defrost in refrigerator overnight and heat for 5-10. They can be eaten at room temperature. You can also microwave them for about 20 seconds, but they won't be crispy. My grandkids in LA will eat them right out of the fridge!

Potato Filling, Patata: (Most common)

3 large potatoes, preferably bakers cooked and mashed (about 4 cups, including instant)
1 1/2 cup grated Parmesan or Romano cheese, plus more for sprinkling
1/2 cup feta
1 tsp. salt
4 large eggs, 1 for basting
Combine the ingredients and mix well.

NOTE: If you want to use instant mashed potatoes: 1½ cups flakes makes 3 cups mashed. Add more cheese if desired. Left over dough? Make boyicos. (See appetizers)

Rice Filling, Arroz: (a favorite of my Auntie Victoria Almeleh and Auntie Glavina Almeleh)

1 cups short-grain rice
3 cups water
1 tsp. salt
1 cup grated Parmesan cheese
8 ounces cottage cheese, about a cup
¼-½ cup feta
5 large eggs, beaten

Rinse the rice and drain. Bring water and oil to a boil and add rice. Bring rice to a boil, reduce heat and cover. Cook about 30 minutes until the water is absorbed. Transfer rice to a bowl to cool. Add the eggs and cheeses. Mix well. Add more salt if desired.

Pumpkin Filling, Calabasa: a sweet favorite for Rosh Hashona)

1 15 oz. can pure canned pumpkin
1small egg, beaten
3 Tbsp. tapioca or more to absorb moisture
½ tsp. cinnamon
1/2 cup brown sugar, packed

Mix all the ingredients well. Let sit 5 minutes before using so tapioca can absorb moisture.

Eggplant Filling, Berengena

1 large eggplant, peeled and cubed
1 tomato, peeled and diced
1 medium onion, chopped
1 tsp. salt

3 Tbsp. vegetable oil
½ cup grated Parmesan or Romano
1 egg

Sauté the onion in the oil and add the eggplant, tomato and salt. Simmer for ½ hour. Cool before adding egg and cheese.

Note: Feel free to reduce filling recipes and make more than one type bureca at a time.
I once got a request for spinach-filled burecas. The boyo filling can be used.

FILLO TRIANGLES/ SAVORY AND SWEET

<u>Fillo (Phyllo)</u> is paper-thin pastry dough. It provides a crunchy delight when baked to a golden brown. Special handling is required to prevent drying out. It can be purchased in any chain store or Cash and Carry in the freezer department by frozen pie crusts and puff pastry shells. Costco does not carry it. It comes in a long 1 lb. box. Not all brands are of the same dimensions, but they are all Kosher.

<u>Working with fillo dough and making triangles:</u>

Allow fillo dough to thaw in refrigerator overnight. Cut away the plastic wrapping. Unroll and lay dough flat on a dry surface. Cover completely with plastic wrap and a cloth/kitchen towel sprinkled with a little water. If you want to make half, divide dough and put it back in the plastic wrap and back in the box. Store in the refrigerator, if to be eaten soon, or freeze for future use.

Pour about a cup of vegetable oil in a bowl and get a basting brush or use spray oil. Oil the working surface. Place one sheet on surface and brush with oil. Get the edges first. Place another sheet on top and brush again. Cut into equidistant strips. The more strips, the smaller the triangles. Place a heaping teaspoon to a tablespoon of cooled filling at the bottom of each strip. Fold one corner diagonally across to opposite edge to form a triangle. Keep folding triangle onto itself tightly and brush outside with oil.

Bake at 350⁰ until golden brown about 20-25 minutes.

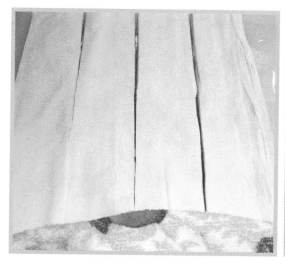

PREPARE FILLO DOUGH

MAKING FILLO TRIANGLES

BAKED FILLO TRIANGLES

Fillings: Any of the above fillings can be used, in addition to the meat filling used for pastelicos below. Adjust quantity to amount of triangles. One pound of fillo makes about 4-5 dozen. You do not need an extra egg for basting. I will add an apple filling which is a favorite for Rosh Hashona. Have your filling(s) ready to go.

Apple Filling:

4 large apples, peeled and diced
¾ cup sugar
½ tsp, cinnamon
2 tbsp. uncooked tapioca

Place prepared apples in a bowl and add the tapioca. Wait a few minutes to let the tapioca expand. Add the rest of the ingredients

Toppings: Use cheese for potatoes or eggplant, sesame seeds for meat and cinnamon-sugar for pumpkin.

PASTELES/PASTELICOS

(Small artisan meat pies)

Makes about 30-40

This recipe is sooo yummy! But it takes a lot of practice. Use lean meat to reduce calories. I got a request to make these with tofu crumbles once. Start with the filling:

2 lbs. lean ground beef
2 onions, chopped
1 tsp. salt
Pepper to taste
½ cup finely chopped parsley

¼ cup oil

2 hard-boiled eggs, chopped (optional)

½ cup tomato sauce (or ½ cup canned tomatoes, well-drained and finely chopped)

¼ cup rice

¾ cup water

Sauté onions in oil until tender. Add ground beef and cook well. (At this point, some just add the seasoning and parsley and skip the rest) Traditionally, add the tomato, salt and pepper. Then add rice and water. Simmer for at least 20 minutes until tender. When cool, add eggs and parsley.

Note: The filling can be made in advance and refrigerated. Pick out some fat, too, if you want.

Dough

1 cup vegetable oil

2 ½ cups water

1 tsp. salt

6-7 cups flour

Topping—1 beaten egg and sesame seeds

Boil oil, water and salt. Measure flour in a bowl, remove water from heat and stir in flour quickly with a wooden spoon. When well blended, knead dough until smooth. You might have to add a little more flour.

Two methods for making the pies: 1.Traditional all by hand 2. With dough press tool and hand

Traditional:

1. Shape dough into large walnut-sized balls with same number of smaller balls for tops.
2. With thumb, shape larger ball into a cup 3" in diameter and flatten smaller balls into about 2" diameter circles, the size of the cup.
3. Place the cup in the palm of your hand and fill it with a heaping teaspoon of filling.
4. Place smaller circle on top and twirl the pie while pressing the edges together firmly upward.
5. Put pie on a surface and flute or pinch it with thumb and forefinger (what I do) or make little slits with a knife, using up and down strokes.
6. Spray oil on a baking pan. Arrange pasteles in rows. Brush with beaten egg and sprinkle with sesame seeds.

Bake in a preheated oven about 425* for 30-40 minutes or until light brown.

With 3 ¾" and 2 ½" dough presses: See pictures below.

CUT OUT PASTELES DOUGH WITH TOOLS

PINCH EDGES TO SEAL AND DESIGN

FILL AND TOP PASTELES WITH HANDS

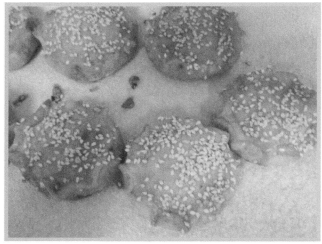

COOKED PASTELES ON A PLATE

1. Roll out a large section of cooled dough to ¼" thickness with a rolling pin.
2. Cut out an equal number of large and small circles with dough presses.
3. Scoop up perimeter dough to be reused.
4. Follow steps 3-6 of the traditional method above.

VARIATION: Use eggplant filling instead of meat.

QUASHJADOS/FRITADAS

DE ESPINACA

Spinach bake recipe for large pan at least 13x9"

2 ½ lbs. fresh spinach, chopped fine (1 Costco bag or 4-5 bunches, frersh or 2 cartons prewashed baby spinach) I do not recommend frozen spinach.
8-10 extra large eggs, beaten
3-4 slices stale bread soaked in water and squeezed dry or 1 c. potato flakes
2 cups grated parmesan or Romano cheese (or some of each)
Optional extra ¼-1/2 c. parmesan for topping
1 cup feta
1 tsp. salt or to taste
2 Tbs. oil to cover pan

Preheat oven to 400*

Chop cleaned spinach (stems removed). Mix everything except oil in a large bowl. Oil the pan. Some heat the oiled pan. Fill the pan, spreading ingredients evenly and filling corners. Sprinkle with more parmesan, if desired. Bake 40-50 minutes or until browned. Cut into squares. Eat it hot or cold. It is also traditionally served with hard-boiled eggs. (See huevos haminados on p.)

VARIATIONS:

1. Substitute fresh spinach with 3-4 packages frozen chopped spinach, completely thawed. Try letting it stand overnight.

2. Use 1 ½ -2 cups liquid egg whites or mix whole eggs with egg whites or use substitute eggs
3. Instead of potato flakes, boil and mash 2-3 potatoes or use leftover mashed potatoes
4. For Passover, 4-5 matzos, soaked and crumbled or ½ cup matzo meal (farfel) with ½ cup potato flakes
5. Use a different hard cheese like asiago, kasseri, or kashkaval
6. Use ½ cup bread crumbs or cracker crumbs

DE ESPINACA: Recipe for small pan like 8x8", 9x9"S

3 bunches spinach, about 1 lb or 2 pkg. frozen chopped
5 large eggs, well-beaten
2 slices soaked and squeezed-dried bread or ½ c. potato flakes or matzo meal
1 c. Parmesan or other hard cheese, grated, more for sprinkling
½ c. feta

1/2 tsp. salt
1 Tbs. oil to cover pan

Preheat oven to 400*. Follow instructions for large pan, but bake about 25 minutes.

CUT QUASHJADO DE ESPINACA

DE ESPINACA CON FONGOS (WITH POTATO NESTS)

2 lbs. potatoes, about 4 large, cooked and mashed
2 ½ lbs spinach
1½ cups grated parmesan
½ c. feta
6 eggs, beaten
½ tsp. salt or to taste
2 tsp. butter
2 Tbs. oil

Mix mashed potatoes with 1 ¼ c. cheese, the salt and eggs. Chop the spinach finely and mix it with HALF the potato mixture. Oil a pan or baking dish and heat in oven for a few minutes at 350*. Pour in the spinach mixture. Make 6-8 equidistant mounds pressed in with the rest of the potato-cheese mixture. Dot with butter and sprinkle the remaining cheese on top. Bake 30 minutes or until browned at 350*. Cut into squares and serve warm.

DE TOMAT

Tomato Bake for 9x13" pan or 3 quart baking dish.

Serves 8-12 depending on cut

3 cans (14.5 oz.) diced tomatoes or 2 lbs. fresh, peeled and diced
2 Tbs. oil
1 Tbs. sugar
½ cup chopped parsley
2 slices soft bread crumbs
6 eggs, well beaten
1 cup grated Parmesan or Romano cheese
½ cup feta, crumbled

Heat the oil in a saucepan. Add tomatoes with liquid and the sugar. Bring to a boil while mashing. Lower heat and simmer until tomatoes are very thick. Let cool when done. Meanwhile, mix all ingredients except eggs. Add to the cooled tomatoes and mix well. Fold in the eggs and pour into oiled pan. Bake at 400° for 45-50 minutes, until firm and brown on top. Cool and cut into serving pieces. Some like it hot and some like it cold!

VARIATIONS:

1. Omit all cheese.
2. Use dried bread crumbs, potato flakes or crushed crackers for filler.
3. Add ½ cup cottage cheese or omit feta and use 1 cup.
4. Sprinkle top with ¼ cup Parmesan as I do.
5. Add ½ cup of chopped onion or green pepper or both.

DE CALABASA

Zucchini soufflé for an 8 or 9" square pan

5 medium or 3 large zucchini, grated raw
2 slices dry bread or 1 mashed potato or 3-4 tablespoons matzo meal
3 large eggs, well beaten
1/2 -3/4 c. Romano or Parmesan cheese, grated
Oil to cover bottom of pan
Optional: 1 tsp. salt and 1 tbsp. parsley

Drain and squeeze thoroughly the grated zucchini. Add filler of choice and other ingredients in a bowl.

Place oil in the pan. Pour in mixture. Bake for 45 minutes at 375° or until browned. Cut into squares to serve 8 or 9.

ORIGINAL QUASHJADO HARAMBUSHJA (A MESS OF INGREDIENTS)

1 lb. chopped spinach
½ cup feta
½ cup sun-dried tomatoes
½ cup chopped onion
½ cup mashed potatoes
4-5 eggs

Mix all together and place in a8 or 9" square greased baking pan. Sprinkle parmesan on top. Bake in a preheated 400⁰oven for 45-55 minutes, or until browned.

HUEVOS (EGGS) AND MY FAVORITE SEPHARDIC BREAKFASTS

All the savory pastries can be served for breakfast. They are usually accompanied by hard-boiled eggs. The special "huevos haminados" take some time to prepare. I usually only make them for Passover.

HUEVOS HAMINADOS (flavored hard-boiled eggs)

Recipe can be doubled or tripled
6 eggs
2 tsp. oil
Outer skin of 3-4 onions
2 tsp. coffee grounds, fresh or used
Water to cover eggs

Place everything in a pan that has a cover. Bring to a boil and boil 1-2 minutes. Reduce heat, cover and simmer for at least 5 hours or until shells are a rich brown or maroon color. Add more water as it evaporates. Drain, rinse shells and refrigerate. The eggs can be reheated in the oven.

HUEVOS HAMINADOS

EGGS AND SALAMI (quantities can vary depending on servings needed)

Spray a large frying pan with oil and heat.

Lay in about 12 slices of salami and brown a little.

Crack 6 eggs over the meat.

Cover and cook to preferred doneness of yolk.

Add salt and pepper to taste. Serve with toast, if desired.

HUEVOS CON TOMAT (Poached Eggs and Tomatoes)

3-4 fresh tomatoes, preferably skinned, sliced or diced or canned equivalent

4-6 eggs

¼ cup crumbled feta or shaved hard cheese like Romano

2 tsp. olive oil or spray

Salt and pepper to taste

Heat some oil in a skillet. Spread out tomatoes and cook a few minutes. Spread cheese over tomatoes. Crack eggs, one at a time, over tomatoes. Cover. Cook to desired doneness of yolks. Season as desired.

Variation: Use spinach, sliced zucchini or kale instead of tomato.

SOOTLACH (Rice Flour Pudding) 6 servings

½ cup rice flour

4 cups (1qrt.) milk

½ -3/4 cup sugar to taste

Cinnamon for sprinkling

Pour milk in a saucepan. Add rice flour and whisk to blend. Add sugar. Cook on medium-high heat while stirring often to avoid lumps or burning. Cook about 20 minutes until thick. Pour into individual bowls or custard cups. Sprinkle with cinnamon. Serve warm or cold.

Notes: I enjoy making cinnamon smiley faces for children. Serve with toasted rosca (See Bread section) or other toast. My grandchildren like to add a little butter and dunk their toast in the pudding. I always serve sootlach to break the fast of Yom Kippur as my Auntie Vickie Almeleh used to do. Sootlach can be eaten for breakfast, dessert, or a snack.

ARROZ CON LECHE (Rice and Milk Pudding) 6-8 servings

1 cup rinsed rice

2 cups water

½-3/4 cup sugar

3 cups milk

Cinnamon for sprinkling

¼ cup raisins (optional)

In a saucepan, combine rice and water. Bring to a boil over high heat. Reduce heat, cover and steam rice until water is absorbed. Add milk and sugar, cooking and stirring slowly over medium-high heat about 30-35 minutes.

Add raisins, if desired. Pour into a casserole dish or individual bowls. Sprinkle with cinnamon. Serve warm or refrigerate for a cold dessert.

MOROCCAN SHAKSHOOKA (Eggs in Tomato Sauce)

Serves 6 for breakfast, lunch or brunch

2 tbsp. olive oil
1 medium onion, diced
1 clove garlic, minced
¼ tsp. turmeric
1 tsp. salt
1 tsp. cumin
½-1 tsp. red chili flakes (hot) or 1 tsp. chili powder (mild)
1 lb. ripe tomatoes, chopped, or 2 cans diced tomatoes
6 eggs

Heat the oil in a large skillet. Add the onion and garlic to sauté over medium heat about 1 minute. Add the other seasonings and cook a few minutes.

Add the tomatoes, stir and cover all to simmer on low heat 10-15 minutes.

Remove cover and crack the eggs, one at a time, over the sauce. Space them evenly. Recover the pan and simmer 5 minutes or until the eggs are cooked to taste.

OTHER BREAKFAST FARE

EGG SOUFFLÈ

2 eggs
2 cups water
1 cup flour
1 cup grated Parmesan
1 tsp. salt
Spray oil

Spray with oil the bottom and sides of a 8 x 10" pan. Beat eggs and one cup water together. Gradually add the flour. Add salt and the second cup of water, continually beating. Mix in the cheese. Pour all into pan and bake 1 hour at 400⁰. Cut into squares and serve.

TORTILLA ESPAÑOLA (SPANISH EGG AND POTATO OMELET)

4 potatoes, peeled and cut into 1/8" slices
4 large eggs
1 large onion, thinly sliced
½ cup oil (mix olive and salad oil)
½ tsp. salt

1. Heat oil in an 8 or 9" skillet. Add potato slice one at a time to prevent sticking.

2. Alternate potato slices with onion slices. Salt the layers a little. Cook over medium heat while lifting and turning the potatoes until they are tender, but not brown.

3. In a large bowl, beat the eggs until foamy

4. Remove potatoes and drain in a colander, reserving 3 tbsp. oil. Add potatoes to beaten eggs. Press down until completely covered. Let stand 15 minutes.

5. Heat 2 tbsp. of the reserved oil in a large skillet until very hot. Add the potato mixture. Rapidly spread it out with a pancake turner. Lower the heat to medium-high and brown. Shake the pan to prevent sticking.

6. When potatoes begin to brown underneath, invert a plate (same size) over skillet and flip the omelet onto the plate.

7. Add 1 more tbsp. of oil to the pan and slide the omelet back in to brown the other side. Lower heat to medium and cook, flipping the omelet 2-3 times more. It should be slightly juicy inside.

8. Serve warm on a platter.

RUM-FLAVORED FRENCH TOAST

4 eggs or 2 eggs and 2 egg whites
2/3 cup milk
1 tbsp. rum flavoring
½ tsp. cinnamon
¼ tsp. salt
¼ cup sugar
Butter for browning
8-10 slices bread, white, French or Challah
Powdered sugar for topping

Whisk the first seven ingredients together in a shallow bowl. Soak both sides of each bread slice, one at a time, in the egg mixture. Brown both sides of the bread in a hot buttered skillet. Serve hot with sprinkled powdered sugar.

SWEDISH PANCAKES

(My ex, Fred Carlbom, had Swedish ancestry and would make these pancakes for the family.)

1½ cups flour
3 cups milk
3 eggs, beaten
½ tsp. salt
¼ cup water
2 tbsp. melted butter
Granulated or powdered sugar for topping

Sift flour and salt into a bowl. Add half the milk and blend. Add the rest of the milk. Beat until smooth. Add remaining ingredients and mix well. Drop by spoonfuls onto a hot greased griddle and brown lightly on both sides. (Or use a special Swedish pancake cast iron pan.) Top with more butter, if desired, and sprinkle with sugar. Stack a few pancakes together or curl each pancake for a bite-size finger-food delight.

BROILED GRAPEFRUIT

2 or more large pink or Ruby Red grapefruit
Butter
Brown sugar
Cinnamon

Wash and cut grapefruits in half crosswise. With a serrated spoon or knife, loosen each wedge. Sprinkle the halves with brown sugar and cinnamon. Dot them with butter. Broil in a baking pan for 5-10 minutes until browned.

VEGGIE OMELET

For 2 servings:

6 eggs or 4 eggs and 2 egg whites or ½ cup egg substitute
1 small onion, chopped, or several chopped scallions
¼ cup green pepper, chopped
1 small tomato, chopped
¼ cup water
Olive oil
1/8 tsp. pepper
¼ tsp. oregano
¼ tsp. salt
½ cup shredded cheddar cheese

Sauté onion and green pepper until tender. Add the tomato, oregano and pepper. Cook until vegetables are tender. Set aside and keep warm. In a bowl, beat the eggs with the salt and pour into a greased skillet. Lift the edges of the eggs to thoroughly cook them. Sprinkle cheese on one half. Add veggies over cheese and fold over the other side. Just cook until cheese starts to melt. Cut omelet in half for 2 servings.

CHEESY EGG WHITE SCRAMBLE

For 4-5 servings:
8-10 fresh egg whites or equivalent from a carton
1/2 cup grated Parmesan cheese
¼ cup feta cheese
Olive oil spray
Salt and pepper to taste

Heat a large nonstick skillet with oil. Mix cheeses with egg whites, salt and pepper. Pour mixture into the skillet and scramble with a wooden spatula to desired consistency.

GLUTEN-FREE BLUEBERRY MUFFINS

2 cups gluten-free flour (I use Namaste Flour Blend)
2 tsp. each of baking powder and baking soda
1 tsp. salt
1 tsp. xanthan gum (Find it in health or natural food section of a store.)
½ cup canola oil
1 tsp. cinnamon
2/3 cup pure maple syrup or agave nectar
2/3 cup rice or almond milk
1 tbsp. vanilla
1 cup fresh or frozen blueberries

Preheat oven to 325° and fill a 12-muffin pan with paper cups.

Mix flour, baking soda and powder, salt, cinnamon and xanthan gum. Add oil, syrup, milk and vanilla.

Gently fold in the blueberries. Fill each paper cup 1/3 full. Bake 20-22 minutes. Let stand about 10 minutes before transferring to a wire rack to cool.

APPLE COFFEE CAKE

3 large eggs
1 ½ cups sugar
1 cup oil
1 tsp. vanilla
½ tsp. salt 2 cups flour
1 tsp. baking soda
1 tsp. cinnamon
3 cups peeled apples thinly sliced
1 cup chopped walnuts
A sprinkling of powdered sugar

Mix sugar, eggs and oil well. Add vanilla, salt, flour, soda and cinnamon. Fold in the apples and nuts. Bake in a greased and floured 9x13 pan for 40-45 minutes. Sprinkle with powdered sugar.

FRUIT SMOOTHIES AND SHAKES

1. ¼ cup unsweetened fruit juice

   ¾ cup frozen strawberries

   4-5 ice cubes

   ¾ cup milk, regular or substitute such as soy or almond milk

   1 tsp. sugar or 1 packet of a sweetener such as Stevia or Truvia

   Combine all in a blender. Add some water if shake is too thick.

2. 1 portion of your favorite protein powder

   1 cup almond milk

   1 tsp. cinnamon

   ½ tsp. turmeric

   ¼ tsp. ginger

   1 tsp. raw honey

   Blend all together.

3. 1/2 cup orange juice

   1/4 cup milk or plain yogurt

   ½ cup ice cubes, crushed

   1 tbsp. sugar

   Blend all together

4. ½ cup vanilla fat-free frozen yogurt

   ¾ cup crushed ice

   ½ of banana

   ¼ cup coconut water

   1 tsp. peanut butter

5. Four servings

   1½ cups milk

   ¼ cup honey

   2 cups vanilla frozen yogurt

   1 cup mixed berries, fresh or frozen, thawed

   Blend all in a blender.

FAVORITE APPETIZERS/SNACKS

(See Passover recipes for more.)

BOYICOS (Cheesy Pinwheels) (I also describe these as Sephardic cheese-its)

Recipe for about 6 dozen

1 cup oil
2/3 cup cold water
1 tsp. salt
4 cups flour
2 cups grated Romano or Parmesan cheese
1 beaten egg for brushing

Mix in a bowl the first 4 ingredients with 1 cup of the cheese. Reserve 1 cup of cheese. The dough should be a bit softer than pie dough. Divide dough into 5 parts. Roll the parts with a rolling pin to ¼" thickness, forming a rectangular shape. Sprinkle with cheese and roll up the dough lengthwise like a jelly roll. Cut into ½" pieces. Lay pinwheel sides up and flatten with the palm of your hand or bottom of a glass.

Brush tops with beaten egg. Sprinkle with more cheese. Bake at 375⁰ for 20-30 minutes.

Variations:

Shape dough into 1" balls. Flatten with tines of a fork and sprinkle cheese.
Use leftover boreca dough and mix with cheese. Follow the rest of steps.
Use leftover boreca fillng to spread on rolled out dough before making pinwheels.

BOYICOS

YAPRAKES (Stuffed Grape Leaves)

28 grape leaves purchased in an 8 oz. jar

MAKING YAPRRKES

COOKED YAPRAKES

Filling mixture:

1 cup short grain pearl rice
2 large or 3 medium onions, finely chopped
¼ cup oil
1 cup water
1 tsp. salt and ½ tsp. pepper
½ cup fresh parsley, minced, or 1 tbsp. dried

Liquid Mixture:

2-3 lemons, juiced
¼ cup oil
1 1/2 cup water
½ tsp. salt

1. Unfold and rinse the leaves. Lay them out flat, shiny side down. (I usually do 6 at a time.) Cut off the stems.

2. Filling: Heat the oil in a large fry pan. Stir-fry the onions until transparent. Add the rice, salt and pepper and 1 cup water. Cook until the water evaporates, about 10-15 minutes on medium heat. Let cool. Add the parsley.

3. Place a tablespoon of the rice mixture in the center of each leaf. Fold the left and right side over the filling and roll tightly in a cigar shape. Arrange closely in a 2-quart saucepan. Form layers.

4. Prepare the liquid mixture and pour over the yaprakes. Cover with any leftover leaves. Cover the pan with a tight fitting lid and cook on low-medium heat for 30-40 minutes until rice is tender. Cool. Refrigerate. Generally served cold.

<u>Oven method:</u> Place yaprakes, seam sides down, in a 13 x 9-inch baking dish, single rows.

Use just ½ cup water in the liquid mixture and pour over yaprakes. Cover and bake at 350* for 30 minutes.

Note: Yaprakes can be frozen. Reheat them with a little water.

AVOCADO DIP

1 large avocado, juice of 1 lemon, 1 tsp. salt and 1clove garlic, minced

Peel and mash the avocado. Add remaining ingredients and mix well. Great with chips!

VARIATION: Add some jarred salsa and voila—**guacamole**!

MEXICAN GUACAMOLE

(My students loved making this recipe in Spanish class)

2 ripe avocados
1 medium tomato, peeled
½ cup finely chopped onion
3 tbsp. finely chopped green chili peppers or hot sauce to taste
1 ½ tbsp. lemon or lime juice
1 tsp. salt
1/8 tsp. pepper

In a medium bowl, crush tomato with a potato masher. Cut avocadoes in half and peel. Slice into tomato and crush until well blended. Add chili peppers, onion, lemon, salt and pepper. Mix well. Refrigerate, covered with plastic wrap, until chilled, about an hour. Serve with corn or pita chips.

TARAMA/GARRO (Red Caviar Dip/Spread)

4-ounce jar red fish roe, about 2 Tbs. (try fish or oriental store)
2 slices white bread, crust removed
Juice of 2 lemons

1/3 cup oil
1 clove crushed garlic, optional

Soak the bread with water. Squeeze dry. In electric mixer, beat the bread and roe, adding the oil, gradually until pink and creamy. Add lemon juice and garlic, if desired. Refrigerate. Traditionally served with crackers or "panderas" (See Breads)

EGGPLANT DIP

2 eggplants
2 tsp. salt,
2 tbsp. oil
2 cloves minced garlic
1 chopped onion

Pierce the eggplants with a fork. Bake in 425* oven until skin shrivels, about 45 minutes. Peel and chop the pulp. Add seasoning and onion. Refrigerate and serve cold.

Note: A chopped red bell pepper or a ripe tomato, peeled and diced, can be added.

Ingredients can be blended in a food processor.

BABA GANOUSH (Eggplant andTahina Dip)

2 eggplants, cooked as in previous recipe
½ cup tahina (paste of ground sesame seeds)
¼ cup olive oil
Juice of 3 lemons
½ tsp. cumin
Garnishes such as chopped parsley and black olives

Chop and mash the pulp of peeled eggplants. Blend in tahina. Add lemon juice, oil and cumin. Serve chilled with pita bread or chips.

HOT ARTICHOKE DIP

1 can or jar of artichoke hearts, drained and chopped
1 cup mayonnaise or Vegenaise
1 cup grated parmesan cheese
1 clove garlic, minced
Garnishes: sliced green onions or chopped tomato, optional

Preheat oven to 350⁰. Mix all the ingredients and place in a 9-inch pie plate. Bake 20 minutes or until lightly browned. Serve with pita or tortilla chips or crackers.

MINI-BOYOS FOR PARTIES (invented by my grandson, Jacob)

Use same ingredients for dough and filling as regular boyos. (See P.) You can cut the recipe in half, depending on how many mini-boyos are desired. Full recipe makes

Make a 1 inch ball with the dough and roll out to 4-5". Place a tablespoon of spinach or other filling in the center and cover by pulling in dough on 4 sides to form a small square or rectangle, approximately 2 ½"x 1 ½". Place on baking sheet sprayed with oil or lined with parchment paper. Sprinkle with grated parmesan cheese. Bake at 400* 20-30 minutes. These can be frozen after cooled.

MINI-BOYOS

DILL PICKLES LIKE MOM MADE

Prep:

You will need jars, lids, cucumbers, garlic cloves and fresh dill.

Sterilize as many jars as you will need by washing them in a dishwasher. Boil the lids. Wash the pickling cucumbers and dill. Clean and cut pieces of fresh cloves of garlic to put in the bottom of each jar. Add a layer of pickles and top with pieces of dill. Add another layer of pickles.

To each jar add:

1 tsp. pickling spices
1 Tbsp. white vinegar
1 Tbsp. salt
1 piece of garlic (optional)
Water

Fill the jars with cold water to about ½ inch from the top. Put lids on very tight. Turn jars upside down and leave on counter overnight. Turn them right side up and tighten the lids again. Store jars in a cool place for six weeks. Chill the pickles before eating.

Note: Use recipe to make pickled green tomatoes.

DEVILED EGGS

6 hard-boiled eggs
2 tbsp. mayonnaise
1 tsp. yellow mustard
¼ tsp. salt
1 tsp. sweet pickle juice or vinegar
White pepper to taste, optional
Paprika for sprinkling

After boiling eggs for 7 minutes, leave them covered in the water about 12 minutes. Rinse them in cold water 1 minute and peel them under cold running water. Pat dry eggs with a paper towel.

Slice eggs lengthwise. Place yolks in a bowl and whites on a serving dish. Mash yolks with a fork and add the next 5 ingredients. Fill the whites and sprinkle with paprika. Refrigerate, covered, if you are not serving the eggs right away.

Note: If you want to get fancy, put the filling in a piping bag with a ½ inch star nozzle and pipe the mixture into the egg whites.

SMOKED SALMON PATÉ

6 oz. smoked salmon
½ cup sour cream
½ cup butter or margarine

2 tbsp. lemon juice
Salt and pepper to taste
½ tsp. chives

Melt the butter or margarine. Place the salmon, sour cream and lemon juice in a blender. Slowly add the butter while mixing. Add salt and pepper. Chill until solid. Shape into a ball and roll paté in snipped chives. Serve with crackers or pita chips.

VARIATIONS: Add 2/3 cup nonfat ricotta and 1 tsp. minced fresh dillweed.

DIPS FOR VEGGIES OR CHIPS

1. CREAM CHEESE AND SOUR CREAM: Blend and add salt and pepper.

2. SPINACH DIP

    1 cup frozen chopped spinach, thawed and drained

    1 cup sour cream

    ½ cup cottage cheese

    1 tbsp. dried onion flakes

    1 tsp. lemon juice

    Salt and pepper to taste

    Combine all the ingredients in a bowl. Chill for 2 hours. Return dip to room temperature befor3e serving.

3. GREEK TZATZIKI (cucumber and yogurt)SAUCE (Also good with fish)

    1 cup plain Greek-style yogurt

    ½ grated and peeled, preferably seedless, cucumber, extra liquid squeezed out

    1-2 cloves garlic, minced

    ½ tsp. coarse salt

    2 tbsp. fresh dill or mint or both

    1 tsp. olive oil

    Mix all ingredients together.

4. GARDEN DIP

    ¾ cup plain yogurt

    ¾ cup cottage cheese

    1 tbsp. minced carrot

    1 tbsp. minced onion

    1 tbsp. minced green bell pepper

    1 clove garlic, minced

    ½ tsp. dried dill weed

Place yogurt and cottage cheese in a blender and mix until smooth. Transfer to a bowl and stir in the other ingredients. Cover and chill.

5. ROASTED RED PEPPER SAUCE (Also good for fish)

    ½ cup roasted red bell pepper

    1 clove garlic

    1 tbsp. balsamic vinegar

    Salt and pepper to taste

    ¼ cup olive oil

    Puree in a blender the first 4 ingredients. Add the oil and continue blending.

PITA CHIPS

4 pita breads (7" diameter), cut into 8 wedges each

Preheat oven to 350⁰. Arrange wedges on 2 baking sheets. Bake until crisp, about 5 minutes. Cook longer for crispier wedges.

SARDINE SPREAD

2 cans sardines in water or oil, drained
2 tbsp. minced onion
½ cup minced celery
1 tsp. lemon juice
4 tbsp. low-fat mayonnaise
1 tsp. Dijon mustard

Mash the sardines and mix with remaining ingredients. Serve on crackers or with pita chips or stuffed celery.

BRUSCHETTA

12 slices from a baguette loaf of Italian or French bread
2 tbsp. olive oil, divided
1 clove garlic, minced
6-8 Roma tomatoes, chopped or 2 cups grape tomatoes, halved
½ sweet onion, finely minced
¼ cup minced parsley
¼ cup pitted black olives, sliced
½ tbsp. balsamic vinegar
Salt and pepper to taste
Combine tomatoes, onion, olives, 1tbsp.oil, vinegar, parsley, garlic, salt and pepper in a bowl. Let stand at room temperature for 30 minutes.

Brush bread slices with the rest of the olive oil. Grill/ broil each side until golden.

Spoon the topping on each toast.

TUNA STUFFED MUSHROOMS

12 medium mushrooms
½ cup drained, minced tuna
½ tsp. minced onion
¼ tsp. salt
Dash of pepper
3 tbsp. butter or margarine
Paprika

Remove centers of mushrooms. Finely chop the stems. Cook stems in a fry pan with butter. Add tuna and cook 3 minutes. Add onion and seasonings. Remove from head. Stuff the caps and place them in a greased baking pan. Bake at 300⁰ for 15 minutes until brown.

GARBANZO PATTIES

1 can garbanzos, also called chickpeas, drained and rinsed
1 clove garlic, minced
½ cup parsley, chopped
1 egg
½ tsp. cumin
½ tsp. salt
½ cup bread crumbs
Olive or canola oil for frying

Puree the garbanzos, parsley, cumin, garlic and salt in a blender. Transfer to a bowl and add the egg and enough breadcrumbs so it is easy to make patties. Form patties and fry in hot oil in a nonstick pan. Cook about 2 minutes per side. Drain excess oil on paper towels.

CHICKEN WINGS

1/3 cup soy sauce
¼ cup firmly packed brown sugar
1 tbsp. cornstarch
2 tbsp. vinegar
1 tbsp. minced ginger root
1 large or 2 small cloves garlic, minced
2 lbs. chicken wings

Cut the tips off the chicken wings and cut through the remaining joint to get two pieces.

Spread the pieces over the bottom of a large shallow dish. Combine the remaining ingredients in a bowl. Pour the mixture over the wings and refrigerate for 1-2 hours. Remove wings from marinade, place on a broiler pan and cook for an hour at 350⁰. Baste twice.

FAVORITE SOUPS and STEWS

LEMONY CHICKEN AND RICE SOUP

Note: This soup was always served at my Aunty Victoria Almeleh's house to break the fast of Yom Kippur. She used cut-up pieces of chicken. I usually use leftover chicken, boiled, cooled and deboned. I remove the skin and save the broth. Frozen chicken can also be used. Frozen vegetables can be thrown in at the end. Recipe makes 4-6 servings.

1 fresh cut-up fryer (to serve six), or cooked leftover chicken pieces/carcass
¼ cup rice
Salt and pepper to taste (Italian seasoning, optional)
4 cups water
1-2 cups chicken broth with leftover chicken
½ cup celery, chopped
½ cup onion, chopped
Juice of 1 lemon or to taste

If using a fresh fryer, sauté it in 2 tablespoons oil for 5-6 minutes. Place chicken in a large pot. Add the water and cook ½ hour. Add the rest of the ingredients and simmer ½ hour or until rice is tender.

Using leftover chicken, boil and simmer chicken with water for ½ hour. Remove chicken and let it cool.

Debone chicken and remove skin if desired. Return chicken to pot and add the other ingredients. Boil and simmer, covered, for another ½ hour. Yummy with toasted rosca! (See Breads)

Variations: Add ½ cup diced tomatoes. Add 1 cup chopped or sliced carrots with the celery. Use noodles or potato instead of rice. Throw in mixed frozen vegetables last 10 minutes.

GREEK AVGOLEMONO/EGG-LEMON SOUP

Serves 4-6
6 cups chicken broth
½ cup short-grain rice
½ cup thinly sliced celery
1 tsp. salt
2 eggs
4-6 tbsp. lemon juice

Boil the broth in a large saucepan. Add rice and salt. Bring to a boil and simmer for 15 minutes or until rice is tender. In a medium-sized bowl, whisk the egg s and lemon juice until frothy.

When the rice is ready, reduce the heat; stir it a bit before slowly adding a few spoonfuls of the broth to the egg mixture, stirring constantly so the egg will not curdle. Repeat.

Slowly drizzle in the egg mixture while whisking and simmering until soup thickens a little. Do not boil more. Soup should appear creamy. Season it with salt and pepper.

Notes: This recipe can be made a day in advance. Cover the soup and refrigerate it. Reheat on low heat. Try adding some cooked boneless chunks of chicken to each serving. Garnish with lemon slices and fresh chopped parsley.

MEDITERRANEAN VEGETABLE SOUP

Serves 6
1 Tbsp. olive oil or spray oil
½ onion, diced
1 can of tomatoes, diced or 1Tbsp. tomato paste
2 cups diced green cabbage
½ cup celery, chopped
½ cup green beans
2/3 cup sliced carrot
½ cup elbow macaroni
½ cup zucchini, diced
Salt to taste
½ tsp. each dried oregano and basil
2 cloves garlic, minced
Juice of ½ a lemon
6 cups water
1 Tbsp. minced parsley, optional

Spray a large saucepan with cooking spray or use oil and heat. Cook the carrots, onion, garlic, and parsley about 5 minutes. Add everything else except the zucchini. Bring to a boil. Reduce heat, cover pan and simmer 30 minutes. Stir in zucchini and heat 3-4 minutes.

Note: This recipe is meatless, but you can substitute some or all of the water with beef or chicken broth.

HOMEMADE TOMATO SOUP

Note: Tomatoes are healthier when cooked!

Recipe serves 4.
2 lbs. tomatoes, chopped or a 28 ounce can of diced tomatoes with juice
1 large onion, sliced thin
1 carrot, chopped
3 Tbsp. tomato paste
3 cups water or chicken broth
2 Tbsp. olive oil
½ cup parsley
2 cloves minced garlic, optional

1 sprig fresh thyme or ½ tsp. dried
1 tsp. sugar
½ tsp. basil
Salt and ground pepper to taste

Heat the oil in a large pot. Add the onion, carrot, garlic, and a sprinkling of salt and pepper. Cook 3-5 minutes until vegetables begin to soften. Add the tomato paste and stir to cover the vegetables. Add the rest of the ingredients. Bring to a boil. Then simmer 20-30 minutes until soup thickens. If it gets too thick, add more water. **Note:** This soup can be pureed in a blender when cool. It can also be frozen.

GREEN SPLIT PEA SOUP

Recipe serves 6-8
2 tbsp. olive oil
2 onions, chopped
2 carrots, peeled and chopped
2 stalks celery, chopped
4 cloves garlic, minced
1 lb. (16 oz. pkg.) green split peas, rinsed
2 bay leaves
1 tsp. dried thyme
3 quarts (12 cups) water or vegetable stock or chicken broth
Salt and ground pepper to taste

In a large pot, heat the oil and sauté the onions, carrots, celery and garlic about 5 minutes. Add split peas, bay leaves and water or stock, plus seasonings. Bring to a boil, reduce heat and simmer for about 1 ½ hours until peas start dissolving and the soup thickens. Remove bay leaves before serving.

SLOW-COOKED GROUND TURKEY SOUP

1 lb. ground turkey
1 carrot, sliced thinly
2 stalks celery, chopped
2/1/2 cups tomato juice
1 pkg. frozen French-cut green beans
1 cup fresh mushrooms, sliced
1//2 cup tomato, chopped
1 tbsp. dried minced onion
1 tsp. dried oregano
1 tsp. dried basil, crushed
1 ½ tsp Worcestershire sauce
1 clove garlic, minced or ½ tsp. garlic powder
½ tsp. sugar
¼ tsp. pepper
1 bay leaf

Cook the turkey, celery and carrot in a large skillet. Drain off fat. Place In an electric slow cooker. Add the rest of the ingredients. Cover and cook for 6 hours on a low setting, or cook on high or 2 ½-3 hours.

Remove bay leaf before serving. (6 servings)

NOTE: Vegetarians can substitute soy crumbles for turkey.

LENTIL SOUP

1 cup dried lentils
4 cups water or broth
¼ cup oil or margarine
1 cup celery, finely chopped
1 onion, chopped
1 small can tomato sauce
1/2 tsp. salt
¼ tsp. ground pepper

Bring water to boil and boil lentils a few minutes and then drain them.

In a large saucepan over medium heat, sauté celery and onion about 10 minutes until vegetables are tender. Add tomato sauce, salt and pepper. Add lentils and water to cover. Bring to a boil, reduce heat and simmer, covered, 15-20 minutes until the lentils are tender.

EASY MINESTRONE SOUP

2 14.5 oz cans stewed or diced tomatoes
2 14.5oz cans mixed vegetables or large pkg. frozen
3 cups chicken, beef or vegetable broth
1 cup bowtie or your favorite pasta
Season to taste

Combine first 3 ingredients <u>without </u>draining the tomatoes. Bring to a boil. Add pasta and simmer 20 minutes.

BLACK BEAN SOUP

1 can (15 oz) black beans
5 cups chicken or vegetable broth
1 cup chopped onions
2/3 cup diced celery
¾ cup diced carrots
½ cup tomato sauce
3 cloves garlic, minced
2 tsp. oregano
1 tsp. salt

½ tsp. cumin

Pepper to taste

Heat the broth in a large pot. Add the rest of the ingredients and bring to boiling. Lower heat, cover and simmer one hour.

GAZPACHO

6 tomatoes, peeled and quartered
1 onion, quartered
½ cup red wine or sherry
1 cucumber, peeled and finely chopped
1 tbsp. olive oil
1 tbsp. lemon juice
1 tbsp. paprika
2 cloves garlic
¼ tsp. pepper
Salt to taste
2 tbsp. fresh parsley or cilantro to garnish

Place half the onions, tomatoes, and wine in a blender or food processor. Liquefy until smooth and pour into a pot. Repeat with the other half, adding the oil, lemon juice, paprika and garlic. Pour into the pot and simmer 10 minutes. Add cucumber and seasoning. Chill. Serve cold with garnish.

NOTE: Other popular garnishes are black olives and sour cream.

PUREED ASPARAGUS SOUP

1 lb. fresh asparagus, ends trimmed and cut in pieces
2 green onions, chopped
1 clove garlic, minced
1 tbsp. butter or margarine
2 cans low-salt chicken or vegetable broth
½ tsp. salt
½ tsp. dried thyme
1 bay leaf
1/8 tsp. pepper
2 tbsp. flour
3 tbsp. water
¼ cup low-fat sour cream, optional
1 tsp. grated lemon peel, optional

Sauté onions and garlic in butter In a large pot. Add broth, asparagus and seasonings. Bring to a boil, reduce heat, cover and simmer 10 minutes or until asparagus is tender. Drain the asparagus, but keep the liquid. Let it cool a bit. Discard the bay leaf.

In a blender, combine asparagus and ½ of the liquid. Process it until smooth. Return the puree and rest of liquid to the pot. Mix flour and water until smooth and stir it into the soup. Bring to a boil. Cook while stirring a few minutes until thickened. Serve with garnishes, if desired.

LEEKY POTATO SOUP

3-4 leeks, cleaned, cut lengthwise and chopped (only white and light green parts)
2 tbsp. butter or margarine
4 medium potatoes, peeled and diced
2 cups chicken or vegetable broth
2 cups water
Dash of marjoram
¼ cup fresh parsley
½ tsp. dried thyme
Tabasco sauce to taste
Salt and pepper to taste

Cook leeks in butter in a large saucepan. Add salt and pepper. Cover and simmer 10 minutes. Add broth, water and potatoes. Bring to a boil and simmer 2-4 minutes. Pour half of the soup into a blender to puree. Return to pan. (If you want all to be creamy, puree the other half) Add marjoram, parsley and thyme plus some dashes of Tabasco. Add salt and pepper to taste.

SOPA DE AVAS (BEAN STEW)

Serves 6
2 cans Great Northern beans
1 lb. stew meat
1 large onion, chopped
3-4 tbsp. tomato sauce
1 tbsp. oil
Salt and pepper to taste
6-8 cups water

Heat the oil and sauté the onion and meat. Add the tomato sauce, water and seasoning. Cover and simmer 1 hour until meat is done. Add rinsed and drained canned beans. Cook 10-15 minutes more.

VARIATION: Use 2 cups shredded rotisserie chicken breast, 2 cans fat-free chicken broth. Add2 packed cups baby spinach after simmering.

SOPA DE LENTEJAS (LENTIL STEW)

Serves 4-6:
1 cups lentils
2 tbsp. oil
1 large onion, chopped
1 lb. stew meat, optional
2 cups boiling water

1/2 cup tomato sauce

6 cups water

1 tsp. salt and ground pepper to taste

Clean and rinse lentils; boil and drain. Heat 2 tablespoons of oil in a sauce pan. Brown the onions and meat. Cover and simmer until meat is tender. Add tomato sauce, water, lentils and seasoning. Cover and cook on low heat for about 30 minutes. Serve with Spanish rice.

STOFADO (BEEF STEW with CARROTS and POTATOES)

1 lb. beef chuck cut in cubes or stew meat

2 tbsp. oil

3-4 carrots cut in pieces

1 clove minced garlic or ½ tsp. garlic salt

3 potatoes, peeled and quartered

½ cup tomato sauce

1 cup water

2 large onions cut in chunks

1 tsp. salt and pepper to taste

Heat the oil in a saucepan and brown the meat. Add the rest of the ingredients, except the potatoes. Bring all to a boil, cover and simmer 30 minutes. Add the potatoes and cook 30 minutes longer.

VARIATION: Season and dredge meat with flour (try shaking in a paper bag) before browning to create a thicker sauce and omit the tomato sauce. Add some thyme.

VARIATIONS: Use bulgur instead of barley. Omit the barley altogether. Use lima beans or white beans or both. Use hot paprika to spice it up. Use chicken instead of beef.

KIFTES DE SPINACA (SPINACH AND MEAT PATTIES)

2 pkg. chopped spinach or ½ pkg. frozen, defrosted and drained

1 lb. ground meat

2 eggs, beaten

2 slices bread soaked in water and squeezed dry or ¼ cup matzo meal

1 tsp. salt and pepper to taste

Oil for frying

½ cup flour

1 egg, beaten

Sauce:

1 small can tomato sauce

1 onion, diced fine

1 clove garlic, minced

1 cup water

Juice of 1 lemon

½ tsp. salt

Combine the first 5 ingredients. Shape mixture into 12 patties. Dip each patty in flour and then, beaten egg. Fry both sides until browned. Make the sauce in a casserole dish or large saucepan. Put the patties in the sauce, overlapping. Heat and simmer with a cover for 30 minutes.

Add water if the rice starts to stick to the pan. When liquid is almost gone, turn off the heat, stir rice with a fork and let stand on the burner a few minutes. Service for four

VARIATIONS: Stir in ½ cup canned, rinsed garbanzos or pine nuts at the end of cooking. Use 2 fresh peeled and diced tomatoes. Add ½ tsp. sugar. Try ½ tsp. pepper. Add ½ cup finely chopped onion to the sauce. Use bulgur or brown rice instead of white rice.

SPINACH AND BEAN STEW

1½ lbs. fresh spinach (preferred) or 2 pkg. frozen chopped spinach
1 onion, chopped
1 large tomato, chopped or 3 tbsp. tomato sauce
Juice of 1 lemon
1 cup water or chicken broth
1 can of garbanzo or Great Northern beans
Oil

Wash fresh spinach, remove stems and chop. For frozen, defrost and squeeze out excess water. Saute the onion in a large pot. Add the spinach, tomato, and beans. Cover and cook on low heat for 20 minutes. Uncover the stew, add lemon juice and seasoning. Cook an additional 10 minutes, adding water if needed.

FAVORITE SALADS

ENSALADA (GARDEN SALAD WITH VINAGRETTE)

2 tomatoes cut in wedges
1 green onion, chopped (optional)
1/2 cucumber, sliced
½ cup each celery and green pepper
Dressing:
¼ cup olive or vegetable oil
Juice of 1 lemon, more to taste
1 tsp. vinegar
1 tsp. salt
Dash garlic powder (optional)

Combine veggies. Mix dressing and toss the salad.

GREEK SALAD

1 head romaine lettuce, torn
2 tomatoes cut in wedges
1 small cucumber, sliced
½ green pepper in rings
1 Tbsp. chopped parsley
3 ounces feta cheese, crumbled
8-10 Greek kalamata olives
A few slices red onion, thinly sliced

Dressing:

3 Tbsp. olive oil
Juice of 1 lemon
1 tsp. salt, ¼ tsp. pepper
1 tsp. red wine vinegar
¼ tsp. sugar or ½ tsp. honey

Combine all salad ingredients and toss with whisked dressing.

Variation: Serve with grilled boneless chicken breast. Add some pepperoncini peppers.

LEVANTINE TABBOULEH (BULGUR WHEAT SALAD)

1/2 cup fine bulgur
¼ cup olive oil
½ cup fresh lemon juice
1 clove garlic, crushed
1 cup chopped tomato, seeded
½ cucumber, seeded and chopped
½ cup green onion s, chopped
1 cup parsley, chopped fine
¼ cup fresh mint or 1 tbsp. dried
Salt and pepper to taste

Soak bulgur for 30-40 minutes in cold water. Drain well to remove excess moisture. In a large bowl, mix bulgur with remaining ingredients. Add more lemon juice if desired. Chill at least 2 hours. Stir before serving.

ISRAELI CUCUMBER AND TOMATO SALAD

2 large tomatoes, seeded and chopped
1 cucumber, seeded and diced
3 scallions or ¼ cup red onion, chopped fine
1 cup green bell pepper, chopped
½ cup red bell pepper, chopped
½ cup radishes, chopped
¼ cup fresh parsley, chopped fine
2 tbsp. olive oil
Juice of 1 lemon, fresh
Salt and pepper to taste

Combine first 7 ingredients in a large bowl. Whisk together dressing ingredients and add just before serving.

VARIATION DRESSING:

½ cup feta
2 tbsp. boiling water
1 tsp. white wine vinegar
3 tbsp. plain yogurt

Mash all until smooth or process in a blender. Pour over vegetables and serve.

TOMATO, CUCUMBER AND FETA SALAD

3 Roma tomatoes, chopped into ½-inch pieces
1 cucumber, seeded and chopped
½ cup pitted kalamata olives, chopped
½ cup feta cheese, crumbled (try low-fat feta if you are watching calories)
1 tsp. grated lemon rind

½ tsp. salt
¼ tsp. ground pepper
1 Tbsp. olive oil, optional

Toss tomatoes, cucumbers and seasoning in a large bowl. Marinate for 15 minutes. Serve topped with feta and olives.

MOROCCAN CARROT SALAD

10-12 carrots (2 lbs.), peeled and sliced into rounds
2 cloves garlic, minced
2 tsp. paprika
1 Tbsp. ground cumin
2 Tbsp. chopped parsley
3 Tbsp. fresh lemon juice
2 Tbsp. olive oil
A few pinches cayenne, to taste
Salt and pepper to taste
A little cinnamon, optional

Boil the carrots in water with a little salt until carrots are tender. Drain and cool. Put them in a large bowl. In a small bowl, whisk the seasoning s together and pour over the carrots. Mix well. Cover and chill before serving. Garnish with additional parsley, if you wish.

Variation: Use vinegar instead of lemon juice. Use fresh cilantro instead of parsley.

Boil potatoes in salted water 15 minutes until tender. Test with a fork. Drain and rinse with cold water. When cooled, cut the potatoes into cubes or quarters. Whisk the vinegar, mustard and then olive oil in a large bowl. Stir in the shallot, parsley and tarragon. Add the potatoes, eggs and celery. Toss and season.

RACHEL'S POTATO SALAD

3-4 baking potatoes, peeled and cut into pieces
3 hard-boiled eggs
½ cup chopped celery
2 chopped scallions
3 radishes, trimmed, sliced thin in rounds
½ cup cucumber chips, diced
6-8 ripe black olives, sliced in rounds
¼-1/2 cup mayonnaise, regular or low fat
1-2 tsp. yellow mustard
Salt and pepper to taste
Paprika to sprinkle

Boil the cut-up potatoes until semi-soft, not mushy. Throw in the eggs to boil or boil separately. Drain the potatoes and rinse in cold water. Turn them out onto a cutting surface. Chop the potatoes to a desired size. Place them in a large mixing bowl. Peel cooled eggs and chop 2 ½, reserving the rest for decoration. Add the chopped eggs and other ingredients to the bowl. (Reserve a few olive and radish rounds for decoration.) Mix all. Mix the mayonnaise and mustard together before adding to the other ingredients. Decorate with sliced egg rounds, olive and radish rounds. Sprinkle paprika on top.

EGGPLANT SALAD

Recipe for 4-6
2 eggplants
1 tomato, diced
1 green bell pepper, diced
2-3 scallions, chopped
¼ cup parsley leaves
¼ cup fresh lemon juice
2 garlic cloves, minced, or 1 tsp. garlic powder
1 tsp. salt and ¼ tsp. pepper

Rinse and dry the eggplants. Preheat oven to 400*. Line a baking sheet with aluminum foil. Place the eggplants on the foil and roast 40 minutes, turning occasionally. When done (soft), rinse the eggplants to easily remove the peel. In a bowl, mash the flesh with the garlic and lemon juice. When ready to serve, add the remaining ingredients. Serve as an appetizer, dip or make a pita sandwich.

BLACK-EYED PEA SALAD/SALSA

A great dish for Rosh Hashona (Jewish New Year) ceremony

1can black-eyed peas
1 can white shoe peg corn
1 bunch green onions, chopped
1 red pepper, diced fine
½ red onion, diced fine
1 jalapeno, seeded and chopped fine
2 avocados cubed (Add only when ready to serve)

Dressing:

¼ cup olive oil
¼ cup red wine vinegar
3-4 cloves garlic, chopped
1 tsp. cumin
½ tsp. lemon pepper
Juice of 1 lime

Combine all ingredients, except avocados. Add dressing and chill. (can be made a day in advance)

Add avocados when ready to serve. Great with crackers!

CARROT RAISIN SALAD

2 cups shredded carrots
1/2 cup raisins
1/4 cup mayonnaise
1 tbsp. orange juice

Combine all ingredients in a bowl and mix well.

VARIATION: Add ½ cup miniature marshmallows or 1 cup diced apple or ½ cup pecans with a teaspoon of honey.

CABBAGE SALAD

6 oz cabbage and carrot coleslaw mix or shred your own mix
2 tbsp. sour cream
1 ½ tbsp. cider vinegar
1 tsp. agave syrup or honey
¼ tsp. salt plus pepper to taste

Mix all together and chill before serving.

TUNA MACARONI SALAD

2 cups cooked elbow macaroni
½ cup chopped celery
¼ cup minced onion
1 7-oz can flaked tuna, drained
Mayonnaise to taste

Mix all together and serve cold or at room temperature.

VARIATION: Skip the tuna and use more macaroni.

FENNEL SALAD

1 large fennel bulb, sliced very thin
2 tbsp. olive oil
1 tbsp. lemon juice
1 tbsp. chopped cilantro or parsley
¼ tsp. thyme
Salt to taste

Mix all together.

VARIATIONS: Add orange or paper-thin apple slices. Add thin onion slices. Top with shaved parmesan.

JICAMA SALAD

1 large jicama
1 tsp. agave or sugar
Juice of 2 lemons
3-4 tbsp. olive oil
2 tbsp. chopped cilantro
6 cups chopped romaine lettuce
Salt and fresh ground pepper to taste

Peel and slice the jicama into sticks. Mix with lettuce and dressing.

TUNA SALAD

2 cans 7oz tuna in water, drained
1 medium onion, red or white, chopped finely
½ cup celery, chopped finely
¼ cup low-fat mayonnaise or more if desired
1 tsp. dried dill weed, optional

Mix all the ingredients together to desired consistency. Chill until ready to serve. Serve on lettuce or in a sandwich or on crackers for an appetizer.

VARIATIONS: Use canned salmon instead of tuna. Add 1 chopped hard-boiled egg. Add chopped pickles of choice. For a salad, top tuna with chopped tomatoes or black olives or both.

EGG SALAD

8 eggs, hardboiled and peeled
½ cup finely chopped celery
½ cup mayonnaise
1 tsp. dried dill weed (optional)
Salt and white pepper to taste

Chop eggs either manually or with a tool such as a salsa maker. Add the remaining ingredients. Serve on lettuce, in a sandwich or with crackers.

VARIATION: Add ¼ small red onion chopped.

MOROCCAN-STYLE CARROT BEET SALAD

4 medium raw beets, greens trimmed to ½ inch
6-7 medium carrots, peeled or scrubbed
1/2 cup parsley
2 tbsp. olive oil
2 cloves garlic, minced
2 tbsp. lemon juice or vinegar

1 tsp. paprika
1 tsp. cumin
½ tsp. Kosher or sea salt
Ground pepper to taste

Boil beets and carrots together in a large pot. Drain and let cool. Peel and trim the beets. Cut them in chunks. Cut the carrots in rounds. Place in a salad bowl.

Prepare the dressing with remaining ingredients and drizzle over the salad. Toss slightly, chill and serve.

MOROCCAN CARROT BEET SALAD

FRUIT SALAD

1 cup apples, peeled, cored and diced
½ cup seedless red grapes cut in half
½ cup celery, diced
1 firm banana cut in rounds
1 orange, peeled, seeded and cut into chunks
½ cup mayonnaise

Combine ingredients and serve chilled or at room temperature.

VARIATIONS:

1. Make it a Waldorf salad by omitting the banana and adding ½ cup walnuts.

2. Make it a fresh fruit salad by omitting the mayonnaise and celery and adding 1 tablespoon lemon juice, 1 tablespoon sugar or honey and seasonal fruits such as cherries, strawberries, etc.

3. Make it an Ambrosia salad by omitting the celery and mayonnaise and adding 1 cup pineapple chunks, ½ cup miniature marshmallows and ½ cup shredded dried coconut.

BREADS

TRADITIONAL AND YEAST BREADS

ROSCA (RING-SHAPED BREAD)

(Rosca, also called "coulouri" by the Jews of Rhodes, was the Sabbath Challah)

2 pkgs. dry yeast or 2 oz. fresh dissolved in 1 cup warm water
8-10 cups flour
3 eggs
¾ cup sugar
½ cup oil
1½ cups warm water
Egg for brushing and sesame seeds for topping

Dissolve the yeast in 1 cup warm water. Pour 8 cups of flour into a mixing bowl. (I use a KitchenAid bowl with a knead attachment) Make a hole in the flour to add eggs, oil, yeast, sugar and the rest of the water. Make dough adding more flour if needed. Knead until dough is smooth and stretchy. Cover bowl with waxed paper or clear wrap sprayed with oil. Let dough rise in a warm place until double in size, about 1 1/2 hours. Punch it down and knead a little. Divide dough into 4-6 pieces depending on desired size of each bread. Roll the dough with your hands into a 2 inch wide cigar shape about 12-14 inches long. (See photo) Bring the ends together to seal and form a ring. With a knife, make decorative slits in the edges about 2 inches apart. Brush with beaten egg and sprinkle with sesame seeds. Place rings on baking sheets lined with parchment paper or baking mats. Make sure they are at least ½ inch apart. Let them rise about 20 minutes before baking until light brown in a 350⁰ oven 20 minutes.

VARIATION SHAPE: Make a 3-braided challah with 3 12-inch ropes.

ROSCA BREAD

ROSCA REINADA (NUT- FILLED COFFEE BREAD)

Filling:

1 lb. chopped nuts

1 cup sugar

1 cup water

1 tsp. ground cinnamon

½ tsp. cloves or to taste

Mix all together to make a soft pasty filling.

VARIATION: Add a few tablespoons of marmalade.

Rosca:

Repeat instructions for ROSCA above. Divide dough again into 4 equal pieces. Roll out each piece into a rectangle about 6x12 inches. Make a 1-inch strip of filling lengthwise in the center of dough. Fold dough by bringing together the edges at the center over the filling. Pinch the edges to seal. With a knife, make small diagonal cuts across the top of the dough for a design. Form a ring by bringing the ends together and sealing with pinches.

Brush with beaten egg and sprinkle with sesame seeds or ground nuts. Place in a floured baking pan, let rise 20-30 minutes and bake 20 minutes at 350⁰ until light brown.

RESHAS OR PANDERICAS (PRETZEL-SHAPED BREADSTICKS)

(This recipe was given to me by my dear cousin Esther Lee Sadis. It makes about 4 dozen reshas.)

5 cups flour
½ cup oil
1½ tbsp. yeast
1½ cups warm water
¼ cup sugar
Topping: 1 beaten egg and sesame seeds

Dissolve yeast in ½ cup warm water.

Mix remaining ingredients and add yeast mixture. Dough should not be soft or sticky. Add more flour if needed. Knead. Let dough rise in a warm place in a covered bowl 1 1/2 -2 hours until double in size. Punch down and let rise again. Pinch off walnut-sized balls and roll into thin strips. Make a pretzel shape by forming a loop and bringing up the ends. Turn pretzel over,, brush with beaten egg and sprinkle on or dip into sesame seeds. Place on a baking sheet lined with parchment paper. Bake at 375⁰ for 20 minutes: then toast a couple of hours at 150-200⁰.

FORMING A RESHA

BAKED RESHAS AND PARMAKS

PANEZIKOS (SWEET ROLLS)

(This recipe is essentially the same dough as ROSCA made into about 2-3 dozen knot rolls)

2 pkgs. dry yeast
2 cups warm water
5-6 cups flour
1/2 cup oil
1/3 cup sugar
2 beaten eggs (reserve 2 tbsp. for brushing top)
Sesame seeds

Dissolve yeast in warm water. Mix together, in a large bowl, the eggs, sugar and oil. Add the yeast mixture and then the flour. Blend thoroughly. Cover and let rise until double in bulk, 1- 1 ½ hours.

Punch down and knead again. Let rise again about 20 minutes. Make rolls in traditional knot shape or other desired shape. Brush with beaten egg and sprinkle with sesame seeds. Place rolls on a floured baking sheet and let rise on pan 10-15 minutes. Bake in a 375⁰ oven 20-30 minutes or until golden brown.

PARMAKS OR BISCOCHADAS (YEAST RUSKS)

(These are traditionally served with Kasseri cheese, Greek olives and coffee. I like to dunk them in coffee. My ex called them dog biscuits.)

1. Dissolve 2 pkgs. dry yeast in 1/3 cup warm water

2. Mix together:

1 1/3 cups water

1/3 cup oil

1/2 cup sugar

2 beaten eggs minus 2 tbsp. for topping

3. Add yeast mixture and 6 ½-7 cups flour

4. Knead dough until smooth. Allow to rise. When double in size, punch down and let rise again.

5. Turn on floured board and knead lightly.

6. Divide dough into 3 parts. Form 12-15-inch ropes (depending on size of your pan) about 1 inch in diameter to fit an oiled rectangular baking pan with a 2 inch edge. Ropes will shrink a bit in the oil, so make them long enough. Place strips side by side to fill the pan. Oil between ropes and let rise about 30 minutes.

7. Brush with beaten egg and top with sesame seeds if so desired. Bake at350⁰ about 30 minutes or until brown.

8. Remove from oven, let cool a bit and then separate ropes. Cut each rope into 4 pieces about 3 inches long. Place pieces on a pan and return to the oven to toast about 3 hours in a 225⁰ oven.

9. Store in an air-tight container.

CHALLAH (A Jewish Sabbath or Holiday Bread)

2 pkgs. dry yeast
2 ½ cups warm water
½ cup honey
4 eggs
1 tbsp. salt
¾ cup oil
9 cups flour
Glaze: 1 egg yolk mixed with 1 tsp. water
Optional topping: sesame or poppy seeds

Preheat oven to 375⁰

Dissolve yeast in water in a large bowl. Add honey and let stand until yeast bubbles. Add salt, eggs and oil. Mix well. Gradually add flour, mixing after each addition. When dough starts to stiffen, knead with floured hands about 6-7 minutes until dough is smooth and pliable and not sticky. Turn dough over often. Let dough rise in a greased bowl until double in size, at least an hour, and then punch it down.

Divide dough in three. Make your favorite shape, usually 3-braided or round. Place on a greased baking sheet and let rise again until double in size, about 20 minutes. Brush with the glaze and bake 45-60 minutes until brown. Cool bread on a rack.

EASY FOCACCIA

1 16 oz, package hot roll mix
1 egg
2 tbsp. olive oil
1/3 cup chopped onion
1 tsp. each of rosemary, basil and oregano
3 tbsp. more olive oil

Grease a 12" pizza pan. Prepare hot roll mix for basic dough and add 1 egg. Use 2 tbsp. olive oil instead of margarine. Knead and allow dough to rest as directed. Roll dough into a 12" round and place in the prepared pan. Cover and let rise in a warm place until double in size, about 30-40 minutes.

In a small skillet cook the onion with the spices until oni9on is tender. Make indentations in the dough with your fingertips. Spread the onion mixture all over. Bake in a 375⁰ oven for 15-20 minutes until golden brown. Cool on a wire rack.

PEASANT BREAD

2 pkgs. yeast
2 cups warm water
1 tsp. sugar
2 tsp. salt
1 tbsp. olive oil

4 cups flour, approximately
Mix the above ingredients and roll out onto a pan

Garlic coating: Coat dough with a mix of 1/3 cup olive oil and 10 cloves garlic, minced

Topping:

½ tsp. lemon pepper
2 leeks, washed and sliced thin
1 cup feta cheese
1 fresh tomato, cubed or 1 small can diced tomatoes
¼ cup parmesan cheese
Oregano, fresh or dried
Spread ingredients over dough.

Bake at 450-475⁰ for 12-15 minutes.

CINNAMON PULL-APARTS

1½ loaves frozen bread dough
¼ cup melted butter or margarine
1 cup sugar
2-3 tsp. cinnamon
1/3 cup light-colored corn syrup

Thaw bread, but do not let it rise. Roll dough into walnut-sized balls. Roll each ball in butter. Mix the cinnamon and sugar together and sprinkle 1/3 of the mixture on the bottom of a greased pan. Line the bottom with the dough balls. Sprinkle another layer of sugar and lay one more layer of dough balls, topped with remaining sugar. Pour syrup over top. Let d9ough rise 30 minutes to an hour. Bake at 350⁰ for 25-35 minutes.

QUICK BREADS

BANANA BREAD

½ cup butter
1 cup sugar
2 eggs
2 tsp. lemon juice
1 cup ripe bananas, mashed
2 cups flour
½ tsp. salt
2½ tsp. baking powder
½ cup walnuts, chopped

Cream butter with sugar and add eggs and lemon juice. Beat well. Alternately add mashed bananas and dry ingredients. Stir in nuts until blended. Pour into a loaf pan sprayed with vegetable spray. Bake at 350⁰ for one hour 15 minutes. The bread is done when a toothpick inserted comes out clean. Cool 10 minutes before serving.

ZUCCHINI BREAD

1 cup sugar
½ cup oil
2 eggs
1 tsp. grated lemon peel
½ tsp. orange flavor (extract)
1½ cups flour
2 tsp. baking powder
½ tsp. baking soda
½ tsp. salt
1/8 tsp. nutmeg
1/8 tsp. ginger
1 cup grated zucchini, unpeeled (Squeeze out excess moisture.)
½ cup nuts, optional

Beat sugar, oil, eggs, lemon peel, and orange flavor until well blended. Sift together all dry ingredients. Add this alternately with the sugar and oil mixture and the cup of grated zucchini. Pour into an oil-sprayed loaf pan and bake at 350⁰ for 55 minutes. Cool in pan for 15 minutes before taking out and serving.

VARIATION: Add ½ cup chocolate chips!

PUMPKIN PECAN BREAD

1 cup canned pumpkin
1 cup firmly packed brown sugar
½ cup canola oil
1 tsp. baking powder
¼ tsp. baking soda
1¾ cups flour
1 ½ tsp. cinnamon
½ tsp. ground ginger
¼ tsp. ground cloves
½ tsp. salt
1 large egg
1 tsp. vanilla extract
½ cup chopped pecans

Preheat oven to 350⁰. Lightly oil and flour a 9x5"loaf pan. Mix together the flour, baking powder and soda and spices in a medium bowl. In a separate bowl, mix the pumpkin, sugar, oil egg and vanilla. Add the dry ingredients just until moistened. Fold in the pecans. Pour all into the pan and bake 55-50 minutes. Let cool in the pan 10 minutes.

GLUTEN-FREE CORNBREAD

1 ¾ cups cornmeal or 1 cup gluten-free flour plus ¾ cup cornmeal
¼ cup sugar
1 tbsp. baking powder
½ tsp. salt
2/3 cup milk
1/3 cup vegetable oil
1 egg

Grease an 8x8" baking pan. Preheat oven to 350⁰. In a medium bowl, mix cornmeal, sugar, baking powder and salt. With a fork, stir in milk, oil and egg just until blended. Pour batter into pan and bake 25 minutes or until golden brown. (Makes 8 servings)

APPLE BLUEBERRY BREAD OR MUFFINS

1/4 cup butter, softened
¾ cup sugar
¼ cup any kind of applesauce
¼ cup apple juice
2 eggs

½ cup regular or almond milk
1 tsp. vanilla
¾ cup flour
1/8 tsp. salt
1 tsp. baking powder
1 cup fresh or frozen blueberries

Topping: 2 tsp. sugar and 1 tsp. ground cinnamon

In a bowl, cream the butter, sugar, apple sauce and the juice together. Beat in eggs, milk and vanilla. Combine the flour, salt and baking powder. Add this to creamed mixture just until moistened. Gently fold in the blueberries. Pour into a greased 9x5" loaf pan or into paper cup lined muffin pan. Bake at 350⁰ for 45-55 minutes until a toothpick inserted near the center comes out clean. Cool for 10 minutes before removing from pan to a wire rack to cool completely.

RAISIN GINGER BREAD

6 tbsp. unsalted butter, softened
½ cup brown sugar
2 tbsp. fresh grated ginger or 1 tbsp. ground
2 tbsp. molasses or pure maple syrup
1 large egg
1 tsp. vanilla
1½ cups flour
2 tsp. grated orange zest

1 tsp. baking powder
1/2 tsp. salt
½ tsp. allspice
¼ tsp. baking soda
½ cup raisins
1¼ cups buttermilk

Preheat oven to 350⁰. Beat butter in a mixer at high speed for 30 seconds. Add sugar, ginger and molasses. Beat 1 minute and add the egg and vanilla.

Combine the flour and the next 6 ingredients. Stir in the raisins. Add the flour and buttermilk alternately and stir until just combined. Pour into a 9x5" loaf pan coated with cooking spray. Bake for 1 hour 15 minutes. Cool in the pan for 15 minutes on a wire rack. Remove from pan and cool completely on the rack.

HOMEMADE BISCUITS

2 cups sifted all-purpose flour
2 tsp. baking powder
1 tsp.alt
¼ cup butter or margarine
¾ cup milk

Sift flour, baking powder and salt in a medium bowl. Cut in the margarine with a pastry blender and knead a few times. Pat out to ½" thick round. Cut into 8 rounds with a2 ½" biscuit cutter or a drinking glass. Re-roll any excess and cut out more biscuits. Bake on a sheet pan at 400⁰ for 15 minutes.

OATMEAL MUFFINS

1 cup flour
1 tsp. baking powder
½ tsp. salt
1 /4 tsp. baking soda
1 cup quick-cooking rolled oats
1 cup buttermilk (or ¾ cup yogurt and ¼ cup milk)
1 egg, slightly beaten
½ cup brown sugar, packed
1/3 cup butter, melted
Optional topping: Additional brown sugar and oatmeal

Line a 12-muffin pan with paper cups. Combine the first 4 ingredients and set aside. Combine oats and buttermilk. Add egg and mix well. Stir in ½ cup brown sugar and butter. Stir in flour mixture until moistened. Spoon batter into muffin cups to 2/3 full. Sprinkle muffins with topping, if desired. Bake at 400⁰ for 18-20 minutes. Cool in cups on a wire rack for 5 minutes.

PASTA AND GRAIN DISHES

ARROZ CON TOMAT (SEPHARDIC PINK RICE)

(My recipe and anecdote was published in <u>Yesterday's Mavens, Today's Foodies</u> by The Washington State Jewish Historical Society, 2011.) My Dad loved this rice with lemony "ensalada". (See Favorite salads)

1 cup long grain rice
2 cups water or chicken broth or half of each
¼ cup tomato sauce or more to taste
2 tbsp. oil
1 tsp. salt

Rinse the rice and drain. Place the water, tomato sauce and salt in a saucepan and bring to a boil. Add the rice, stir and bring to a boil again. Cover, reduce heat and simmer 20 minutes or so, adding more water if the rice starts to stick to the pan. When liquid is almost gone, turn off the heat, stir rice with a fork and let stand on the burner a few minutes. Serves 4

VARIATIONS: Stir in ½ cup canned, rinsed garbanzos or pine nuts at the end of cooking. Use 2 fresh peeled and diced tomatoes. Add ½ tsp. sugar. Try ½ tsp. pepper. Add ½ cup finely chopped onion to the sauce. Use BULGUR or brown rice instead of white rice.

FIDEOS (TOASTED VERMICELLI OR ANGEL HAIR PASTA)

1 8 oz. pkg. fideo (coiled pasta or thin angel hair pasta)
3 tbsp. oil, olive or salad
3 cups water
1/3 cup tomato sauce
1 tsp. salt

Spread the pasta on a baking sheet and toast in oven until golden brown. (Coils can be pan-fried) Combine the water, oil, tomato sauce and salt in a saucepan and bring to a boil. Add the pasta, cover and simmer 10-15 minutes until water is evaporated. Check to see if more water is needed and stir with a fork to keep coils or noodles from sticking. When done, remove from heat, add a little water, stir and let stand, uncovered, about 5 minutes before serving.

Note: Gluten-free pasta can be used: try quinoa or rice varieties.

FIDEOS

MACARON REYNADO (MACARONI AND MEAT)

1 lb. ground beef
¾ cup elbow macaroni
½ cup chopped onion
3 tbsp. parsley, chopped
5-6 eggs
1 tbsp. oil
1 tsp. salt
Pepper to taste

Cook macaroni according to package directions. Rinse and drain. Sauté the meat and onion in oil and add salt and pepper. Beat eggs and add to meat. Add the macaroni and parsley. Pour all into a greased 9x9" pan. Bake 30-40 minutes at 375⁰ until browned. (Optional: Two extra beaten eggs on top before baking.)

SOPA DE FIDEOS/ NOODLE SOUP

1 pkg. (7 oz) angel hair pasta
1 can (14 oz) diced tomatoes
1 large onion, chopped
1-2 cloves garlic, minced
2 Tbsp. olive oil
3 cans (14 oz) chicken broth
1 Tbsp. cilantro, chopped

Salt and pepper to taste
Parmesan for sprinkling on top

Mix tomatoes, onion and garlic in a blender until smooth. Heat the oil in a skillet. Break the pasta into small pieces and brown over medium heat. Stir often until all is golden brown. Set aside.

Combine the blended tomatoes, broth and noodles in a medium pot. Add salt and pepper. Bring to a boil. Reduce heat and cook about 8 minutes. Add cilantro and cook 2 more minutes or until noodles are done. Sprinkle with cheese.

MACARONI AND CHEESE

1 pkg. (8 oz.) elbow macaroni
½ cup milk
2 tbsp. margarine
4 large eggs
½ cup grated Parmesan cheese
1 cup grated American or cheddar cheese
Salt and pepper to taste

Cook macaroni according to package directions. Beat eggs well. Add macaroni, Parmesan, milk and seasonings. Pour into a greased 9x13" pan. Dot the macaroni with margarine and sprinkle with the other cheese. Bake at 400⁰ for 35 minutes until lightly browned.

PASTA with TOMATOES and FETA

4 cups chopped tomatoes
1 tbsp. olive oil
1 tbsp. red wine vinegar
1 clove garlic, minced
2 tbsp. fresh basil, chopped or 1 tbsp. dried
¼ tsp. salt
1/8 tsp. crushed red pepper
¼ cup crumbled feta
4 cups angel hair pasta, cooked

Combine all ingredients except feta and pasta and let stand 10 minutes. Pour over pasta and sprinkle with feta.

ALETREA (PLAIN SPAGHETTI)

½ lb. (8oz) spaghetti or linguine
2 tbsp. olive oil or melted margarine
Grated parmesan to taste

Boil spaghetti according to package directions. Drain and toss with olive oil. Sprinkle with parmesan.

VARIATION: Add 1 tbsp. lemon juice, tsp. garlic powder and fresh or dried basil leaves.

SLOW-COOKER SPAGHETTI SAUCE

(Feeds 12 people)

1 lb. lean ground beef or turkey
2 medium onion s, chopped
1 cup sliced fresh mushrooms
1 medium green pepper, chopped
2 cloves garlic, minced
1 can (14 ½ oz) diced tomatoes, not drained
1 can (12oz) of tomato paste
1 can (8oz) of tomato sauce
1 cup ketchup
½ cup beef or vegetable broth
2 tbsp. Worcestershire sauce
12 cups cooked spaghetti

In a large nonstick skillet, cook the meat, onions, mushrooms, green pepper and garlic over medium heat. Make sure meat is no longer pink! Drain. Transfer to a slow cooker. Stir in the tomatoes, tomato paste and sauce, and ketchup. Mix well. Cover and cook on low for 4-5 hours. Serve over spaghetti.

GOULASH (MEAT, PASTA AND TOMATO)

1 lb. ground beef
1 medium mild white onion, diced
2 small cans tomato sauce
1 can of low-salt tomato soup
2 cups dry elbow macaroni, wheat or gluten-free h(I use brown rice pasta)
2 tbsp. olive oil, divided
1 tsp. salt or to taste
Pinch or oregano

Fry onions and meat with 1 tablespoon oil over medium heat. Cook macaroni separately according to package directions. Drain only partially. Add olive oil and salt, meat and onion mixture and all tomato ingredients. Cook over low heat for approximately ½ hour. When nearly done, add a pinch or oregano.

ALL IN ONE SPAGHETTI AND MEAT

1 lb. ground beef
1 tsp. salt, divided
1 quart tomato juice
¾ tsp. sugar
¼ tsp. pepper
1 clove garlic, minced
1 package spaghetti (6-8 oz)

Cook meat in a large pot or fry pan that has a cover. Add half the salt and cook until red color is gone.

Combine and add the tomato juice and seasonings. Break the spaghetti kin pieces and add, stirring thoroughly. Bring to a boil, cover and reduce heat to a low simmer. Cook 25-30 minutes.

COUSCOUS WITH SPINACH AND TOMATOES

1 ½ cup couscous
3 cups vegetable broth
1 tbsp. olive oil
1 ½ cups of cherry tomatoes, cut in halves
2 cloves garlic, minced
¼ cup fresh spinach, chopped
1-2 shallots, minced
1 tbsp. fresh basil or 1½ dried
Salt and pepper to taste

Bring broth to boil in a large pot. Remove quickly and add couscous, salt and pepper. Stir and cover to let stand a few minutes until liquid is gone.

Heat oil in a fry pan and sauté the tomatoes, spinach, garlic and shallots 3-4 minutes. Add basil and toss. Add salt and pepper. Stir couscous with a fork, place in a bowl and add tomato mixture.

FETTUCCINI WITH SMOKED SALMON

1 cup vegetable broth
3 cups water
1/2 lb. fresh or dried fettuccini or spinach fettuccini
1 tbsp. grated lemon
1 cup nonfat sour cream
1 tbsp. cornstarch
1/3 lb. smoked salmon, cut into small pieces
2 tbsp. fresh dill or 2 tsp. dried

In a large pot, bring to a boil broth and water. Add fettuccini and cook to al dente about 7 minutes.

Blend the cornstarch with 3 tablespoons water and add the sour cream. Stir into the pasta and bring to boil again. Add salmon, dill and grated lemon. Stir gently until hot.

VARIATIONS: Add ¾ cup parmesan cheese. Add cut tomatoes, red pepper or mushrooms, fresh or sautéed.

STIR-FRIED RICE

3 cups cooked rice, white or brown, cooled
3 green onions, chopped
3/4 cup frozen peas, defrosted
½ cup bell pepper, diced, or other preferred vegetable, such as mushrooms or carrots
1 egg, lightly beaten

1 tbsp. canola or sesame oil or spray oil

2 tbsp. low-sodium soy sauce

¼ tsp. salt

1 tsp. ginger

1 tsp. sesame seeds, (optional)

Prepare rice according to package directions. Spray and heat cooking spray in a large non-stick skillet. Cook beaten egg until soft-scrambled. Remove from pan and reserve. Add oil and stir- fry green onions, ginger and bell pepper 3 minutes. Add cooked rice, salt, soy sauce, and peas. Cook until well-heated. Add the scrambled egg. Heat thoroughly and stir often. Top with sesame seeds, if desired.

BROWN RICE WITH BLACK BEANS

1 cup raw brown rice

½ onion, chopped

½ bell pepper, chopped

1 clove garlic, minced

1 cup black beans, rinsed and drained

½ cup vegetable or chicken broth

½ tsp. cumin

1 tbsp. fresh cilantro, chopped

2 tsp. olive oil

Prepare rice according to package directions. Heat the oil on medium heat in a sauce pan, preferably nonstick. Cook onion, pepper and garlic about 5 minutes. Add the beans, broth and cumin. Cook about 15 minutes. Add the cilantro and cook a few minutes more. Serve beans over rice.

BULGUR WITH GARBANZOS

1 cup bulgur

1 onion, chopped fine

3 tbsp. oil

2 cups water

1 tsp. salt

¼ cup tomato sauce

¾ cup canned garbanzos, rinsed and drained

Heat the oil and sauté onion. Add water, salt and tomato sauce. Bring to a boil. Add bulgur and garbanzos. Bring to a boil again, lower heat, cover and simmer for 20 minutes.

PREHITO (BULGUR PUDDING)

(Traditionally served on the Jewish holiday Tu b'Shevat, New Year of Trees)

1 cup bulgur

4 cups water

1/8 cup honey

1 cup ground walnuts
½ cup sugar
1 tsp. cinnamon plus more for sprinkling
½ tsp. salt

Cook bulgur and water on medium heat for 30 minutes, stirring constantly. Add sugar and salt. Cook 10 more minutes. Remove from stove and add honey, cinnamon and ½ the walnuts. Dust a 9x9" pan with cinnamon. Pour in bulgur mixture with remaining nuts. Sprinkle with a little more cinnamon. Cool and cut into squares to serve at room temperature or cold.

VEGGIE RICE PILAF

1 tsp. olive oil
½ cup diced onion
½ cup shredded carrot
½ cup diced celery or ½ cup diced zucchini
1 cup long grain white rice, washed and drained
2 cups chicken broth, regular or gluten-free
½ tsp.sea salt
¼ tsp. pepper
¼ cup chopped parsley

Heat a medium saucepan and cook the vegetables on medium-high heat until tender, about 3 minutes. Add broth, salt and pepper. Bring to a boil on high heat: add rice and reduce heat. Cover and simmer for about 20 minutes or until liquid is absorbed. Remove from heat, stir in parsley and let stand 5 minutes before serving.

CHEESY RICE CASSEROLE

3 tbsp. butter or margarine
1 small onion, chopped fine
1 bunch chopped fresh kale or a frozen pkg., defrosted and drained
1 cup milk, any kind
3 eggs
1 cup shredded sharp cheddar
1 cup shredded low-fat mozzarella
½ cup parmesan and more for topping
3 cups cooked rice
1 tbsp. chopped parsley
1 tsp. each of basil, thyme
Salt and pepper to taste

Preheat oven to 350⁰. Grease a large casserole dish with 1 tbsp. of the butter. On medium-high heat, sautonion in a skillet and add the kale, cooking about 3 minutes. Set aside. In a large bowl, mix milk and eggs together. Add cheeses, rice, parsley, seasonings and kale mixture, mixing well. Pour into the casserole dish and top with parmesan. Bake for 30 minutes and serve hot.

COMIDAS (SEPHARDIC MAIN DISHES)

REINADAS (MEAT-STUFFED VEGETABLES)

STUFFED TOMATOES (TOMAT REINADO)

6 fresh tomatoes
1 lb. hamburger
2 tbsp. parsley, finely chopped
1 egg
1/8 cup raw rice
½ tsp. pepper
1 tsp. salt
1 tbsp. water

½ tsp. sugar
½ cup flour for dipping
1 beaten egg for dipping
2 tbsp. oil for browning

Cut off the tops of the tomatoes and scoop out the pulp. (Try using a serrated spoon.) Keep pulp for later use. Combine the next 6 ingredients well. Stuff the tomatoes.

Dip the meat side of the tomatoes, first in flour and then the beaten egg. Heat oil and brown the tomatoes. Place the reserved pulp in the bottom of a baking dish and arrange the tomatoes on top, meat side up. Sprinkle with sugar. Bake until browned in a 350° oven or leave the tomatoes in the pan to cook on the stove until done.

Variations: Use ground turkey. Stuff red, or green peppers. For variety, stuff 2 or 3 different vegetables together and line dish with the parts of all the vegetables not stuffed.

STUFFED ONIONS (CEBOYAS REINADAS)

6 large onions or 9 medium
3 tomatoes, chopped, or 1 can diced tomatoes, or ½ cup tomato sauce
1 cup water
Same stuffing as above for tomatoes
Flour and egg, for dipping
A pinch of sugar

Prepare the filling. Cut onions in half lengthwise. Remove center layers, leaving last 2 layers for stuffing. Chop the smaller center layers. Fill the larger layers with the meat mixture. Dip in flour and egg. Fry meat side until browned. Then fry the other side a little. Line a baking dish with chopped onion centers. Place the stuffed on ions on top. Make a sauce with the tomatoes and water. If only using tomato sauce, add with the water. Pour sauce over onions and sprinkle with sugar. Cover and bake in a 325⁰ oven 1 hour. Add more water if the sauce gets too thick. (Traditionally served with Spanish rice)

STUFFED CABBAGE LEAVES (YAPRAKIS DE COL)

1 large head of cabbage
1 large onion, chopped

Filling:

1 lb. hamburger
1/2 cup raw rice, rinsed
1 tbsp. parsley, chopped (optional)
1 tsp. salt
Pepper to taste
2 tbsp. water

Sauce:

4 tbsp. lemon juice
1 tbsp. oil
1 cup water
½ cup tomato sauce
Salt and pepper to taste
1 tsp. sugar

Cook the cabbage head in boiling water for 5-10 minutes. Drain. Separate the leaves and choose inner ones that are most tender. Cut off the core and chop with outer leaves. Line a 2-quart saucepan with the chopped onion and chopped cabbage.

In a bowl, mix the filling ingredients. Place a tablespoon or so of filling on each leaf. (If a leaf is very large, cut it in half) Roll the leaf and tuck in the edges. Try using a toothpick to hold it together. Place all the rolled leaves in a pot. Combine sauce ingredients and pour over the stuffed leaves. Bring all to a boil, reduce heat and simmer about 1 hour. Cabbage should be tender when done.

STUFFED ZUCCHINI

6 medium zucchini
1 small onion, diced
1 tbsp. oil
Sprinkling of sugar

Filling:

1/2 lb. ground beef
¼ cup raw rice
1 clove garlic, minced
1 tbsp. chopped parsley, optional
Salt and pepper to taste
1 tbsp. water

Sauce:

1 cup tomato sauce
½ cup water
½ tsp. salt
1 tbsp. oil
2 tbsp. lemon juice, optional

Prepare the filling by mixing meat, onion, garlic salt and pepper.

Cut the tops off the zucchini. Peel and wash. Cut them in half lengthwise. Scoop out the pulp with a small measuring or serrated spoon. Reserve it. Cut zucchini into 3-4 inch pieces and stuff.

Heat 1 tbsp. of oil in a saucepan and sauté the diced onion. Add the pulp. Arrange the stuffed zucchini on top. They can be layered. Mix the sauce ingredients and pour over the zucchini. Sprinkle with sugar. Cover and cook over low heat for an hour or until the zucchini is tender.

Variation: Bake recipe in the oven 1 hour at 350^0.

YAPRAKIS CON AVAS (MEAT- STUFFED GRAPE LEAVES WITH BEANS)

Leaves and Beans:

1 8 oz. jar of grape leaves, rinsed and drained, stems removed

> (If you use fresh leaves, wash and parboil them and drain on paper towels)

2 cans Great Northern beans rinsed and drained (or 1 cup dried boiled for 30 minutes)

Filling:

1 lb. ground beef
¼ cup rice, rinsed and soaked in warm water ½ hour
¼ cup chopped parsley
1 tsp. salt and pepper to taste
1 tbsp. lemon juice
1 tbsp. oil
2 tbsp. tomato sauce

Sauce:

¼ cup tomato sauce
2 cups water
2 tbsp. oil
Juice of 1 lemon, added at the end of cooking

Prepare leaves as described above. Mix the filling ingredients together. Spread out a leaf, shiny side down. Place a teaspoon of the filling by the stem edge. Fold the outer parts of the leaf over the meat and roll it up tightly like a cigar. Repeat for the rest of the leaves.

Layer the beans and yapraks in a sauce pan. Start and end with the beans. Place the yapraks close together so they will not unravel. Prepare the sauce minus the lemon juice. Pour over the yapraks and beans. Cover and cook slowly over medium heat for an hour or until tender. Add the lemon juice the last few minutes. Serve with crusty bread to soak up the "caldu" (sauce).

OTHER FAVORITE MAIN DISHES

KIFTES DE CARNE (MEAT PATTIES in TOMATO SAUCE)

1 lb. ground beef or lamb
1 beaten egg
1 onion, finely chopped
2 slices white bread, soaked and squeezed, or ¼ cup matzo meal
1 tbsp. chopped parsley
1 tsp. salt and pepper to taste
½ cup flour, 1 beaten egg and oil for frying

Sauce:

1 8 oz. can tomato sauce
1 cup water
¼ cup lemon juice
Salt and pepper to taste
1 minced clove garlic

Combine first 6 ingredients. Make 10-12 patties. Dredge each patty with flour and dip in beaten egg.

Heat some oil and fry the patties on both sides until they are golden brown. Mix the sauce and place it in a large saucepan or baking dish. Put the patties in the sauce. It's okay if they overlap. Bring all to a boil, cover and simmer for about 30 minutes.

PORCUPINE MEATBALLS

1 ½ ground beef
½ cup rice
1 can tomato soup, 10 ¾ oz.
1 tsp. salt
½ tsp. pepper
1 tbsp. minced onion
½ cup water

Wash rice. Combine the meat, rice, salt, pepper and onion. Make small meatballs about size of golf balls. Heat the tomato soup and water in a saucepan. Add the meatballs. Bring to a boil, cover and simmer on reduced heat about 30 minutes or until meat is done.

MOUSSAKA (EGGPLANT AND MEAT CASSEROLE)

6-8 servings

2 medium eggplants
2 eggs, beaten
1 onion, chopped
2 tbsp. parsley, chopped
Oil for frying

Meat mixture:

1 lb. ground beef
Salt and pepper to taste
2 tbsp. rice
1 egg

Sauce:

¼ cup water or chicken broth
¼ cup tomato sauce

Wash, peel and cut the eggplants lengthwise ½ inch thick. Soak in salted water 10 minutes. Heat some oil in a fry pan. Dip slices into the egg and fry on both sides until browned. Remove slices to a paper towel to absorb excess oil. In the same pan, sauté the onion and parsley. Remove from the pan and then brown the meat mixture.

Line a greased baking dish with half the eggplant slices. Combine the meat with the onion and parsley and layer it over the eggplant. Top with the rest of the eggplant. Make sauce and pour over all. **Bake at 350⁰ for 1 hour.**

VARIATION: Sauté a large baking potato sliced thin with the onions. Omit the parsley. Slice 3 tomatoes or use 2 cups canned. Layer the eggplant, meat, tomatoes, onion and potatoes in a baking dish sprayed with oil. Pour tomato sauce over all and bake.

VEGETARIAN MOUSSAKA

3 eggplants
2 tsp. salt
¼ cup oil
3-4 garlic cloves, minced
8 oz. can tomato sauce
1 cup water
2 beaten eggs
2 cups mozzarella, shredded

Cut the eggplants lengthwise into 3-4 equal slices. Sprinkle with salt. Let stand for 20 minutes. Pat slices dry with a paper towel. Heat a little oil and fry the garlic 2 minutes. Add the tomato sauce and water. Simmer over low heat 10-25 minutes.

Heat the rest of the oil in a skillet. Dip the eggplant slices into the eggs and fry on both sides until browned. Linea baking dish with part of the eggplant. Pour over ½ cup of the sauce. Sprinke ¼ cup mozzarella on top. Repeat 2 more times ending with cheese. Bake in a 350⁰ oven ½ hour. Great with rice or spaghetti!

EASY POT ROAST

3-4 lb. chuck or pot roast
2 tbsp. onion soup mix
3 tbsp. dry red wine
½ cup tomato juice
2 tbsp. honey
1 bay leaf
Vegetables of your choice, optional

Place meat in the center of a wide piece of heavy aluminum foil in a roasting pan. In a bowl combine onion soup and wine. Blend in tomato juice and honey. Pour over roast and add bay leaf. Wrap foil loosely around meat and seal edges to form air-tight package. Heat oven to 325⁰ to slow cook Bake roast 45 minutes per pound, about 4 hours. Skim off fat id desired. Remove and slice.

Gravy: Thicken juice with flour dissolved in a small amount of water.

BEEF AND BROCCOLI STIR-FRY

½ cup low- salt soy sauce
2 tbsp. lemon juice
1 tbsp. cornstarch
1 tbsp. packed dark brown sugar
1 clove garlic, minced
1 tsp. pepper

1 ½-2 lbs. skirt steak, cut into strips
2 tbsp. vegetable oil, divided
1 medium onion, sliced thin
2 medium heads broccoli, cut into florets
1 tsp. ginger

In a small bowl, combine first 6 ingredients and set aside. Heat one tablespoon of oil in a large skillet or wok on medium-high heat. Add meat and stir fry until almost thoroughly cooked. Transfer meat to a plate and keep warm with a cover. Heat the remaining oil. Add onion and stir-fry 5 minutes. Add broccoli with ½ cup water. Bring to a boil, cover, reduce heat and simmer 3-4 minutes. Return beef to skillet with soy sauce mixture. Add ginger, bring to a boil and cook 2 minutes, stirring constantly until sauce thickens.

TERIYAKI FLANK STEAK

(This recipe was given to me by my nephew, Maynard Lipp)

1 ½-2 lb flank steak for 6-7 servings

Marinade:

4 tbsp. sesame seeds
6 tbsp. vegetable oil
½ cup soy sauce
½ tsp. garlic powder
½ tsp. Pepper
½ tsp. ginger
4 tsp. brown sugar

Trim fat from steak. Place steak in a zip-lock plastic bag and set in a shallow dish.

Combine ingredients for marinade in a small bowl. Pour over steak and seal bag. Marinate in the refrigerator for 8-24 hours. Turn the bag occasionally. Drain steak. Reserve the marinade.

Place steak on a broiler pan rack. Broil 3-4 inches from the head until done to desire. (Allow 12-14 minutes for medium doneness.) Turn once and brush occasionally with reserved marinade.

Pour remaining marinade into a small saucepan. Boil 1 minute. Slice steak thinly against the grain. Serve with the hot marinade.

CHILI CON CARNE

2 tbsp. oil
1 lb. ground beef
1 large onion, chopped
3 cups canned red beans
3 ½ cups canned tomatoes
1-2 tbsp. chili powder
1 tsp. cumin
2 tsp. salt
½ tsp. pepper
1-2 cloves garlic, minced

Fry meat and onion in oil. Add remaining ingredients. Bring to a boil, cover, reduce heat and simmer slowly for about 35 minutes.

MEAT LOAF

1 ½ lbs. lean ground beef
½ cup ketchup
1/3 cup Worcestershire sauce

Salt and pepper to taste
2 eggs
1 cup dry plain bread crumbs
1/3 cup chopped onions
2 tbsp. prepared mustard

Topping:

¼ cup ketchup
¼ tsp. mustard
1 tsp. brown sugar

Combine in a large bowl ketchup, Worcestershire sauce, salt and pepper,, eggs, bread crumbs, onions and mustard. Add ground beef and mix well. Line a 9x5" loaf pan with foil and stuff with the meat mixture. In a small bowl, mix the topping ingredients. Spread over the meat loaf. Bake at 400⁰ for about 45 minutes until done. Drain off fat and let meat loaf stand about 5 minutes before serving.

MEATBALLS AND MARINARA SAUCE

MEATBALLS

2 eggs
1 cup dry bread crumbs
½ cup onions, chopped fine
1 ½ tsp. salt
1 tsp. Worcestershire sauce
½ tsp. pepper
2 lbs. lean ground beef

Beat eggs in a large bowl. Add the onion and seasonings. Then add the beef. Mix well. Shape into 1 ½" in diameter balls to make about 50. Place balls in large ungreased baking pans in single layers. Bake at 400⁰ for about 15 minutes or until done, no longer pink. Turn balls often. Drain and set aside. You can freeze some in a plastic bag for a future meal. Serve with hot bottled marinara sauce if you are in a hurry or make your own as follows.

HOMEMADE MARINARA SAUCE

1 tbsp. olive oil
1 cup diced onion
¼ cup diced green pepper
4-6 cloves garlic, minced
1 large jar (28 oz) crushed tomatoes or crush your own from diced, stewed or fresh tomatoes
1 tsp. sugar or a sugar substitute
¼ cup parsley, chopped
1 tsp. oregano
1 tsp. dried basil
½ tsp. dried rosemary
½ tsp. pepper

Salt to taste
1 bay leaf
½ cup dry red wine, optional

Heat olive oil in a medium pot and sauté the onion, bell pepper and garlic about 5 minutes. Add remaining ingredients and bring to a boil. Cover, reduce heat and simmer 30 minutes. Stir occasionally. Six servings.

BEEF SHORT RIBS IN A COOKING BAG

3-4 lbs. beef ribs, cut into serving size
½ cup flour, divided
1-2 cups BBQ sauce
½ cup each, onion, celery and green pepper
1 tsp. salt
Pepper to taste

Preheat oven to 350⁰. In a cooking bag, place 1 tablespoon flour and shake. Pour in the BBQ sauce and stir. Trim excess fat off the ribs. Combine rest of flour and seasonings. Rub this into the ribs. Place ribs and vegetables in the bag and follow cooking bag instructions. Cook about 2 ½ hours.

CORNED BEEF AND CABBAGE

1 3 lb. corned beef with a spice packet
1 head of cabbage cut in quarters or wedges

Place beef in a large pot. Cover with water and add the spice packet. Boil and then simmer 50 minutes per pound or until tender. Add cabbage and cook 15 minutes more. Remove meat and let rest 15 minutes. Slice across the grain. Serve with cabbage and broth from the pot.

BRISKET WITH WINE

3 lb. brisket
½ cup dry red wine
½ cup ketchup
1 large onion, sliced
3-4 carrots, scrubbed and cut into chunks
4 potatoes cut in chunks, optional
2 cloves garlic, minced
¼ cup brown sugar
1 tsp. Worcestershire sauce
Salt and pepper to taste
1 bay leaf
2 cups water or broth
Place brisket in a large roasting pan or slow cooker. Combine remaining ingredients and pour over meat. Cover tightly. Roast in oven at 300⁰ for 5-6 hours or in slow cooker 6-8 hours.

VEAL SCALOPINE FOR FOUR

1 lb. leg of veal, sliced 1/8" thick or 4 cutlets cut 1/8" thick
4 tbsp. margarine
Pinch of thyme
1 cup Madeira or Sauterne wine
2 tbsp. lemon juice
Flour, seasoned with salt and pepper

Cut meat into serving-size pieces. Roll in seasoned flour. Heat the margarine in a heavy frying pan and brown meat. Lower heat and add wine, lemon juice and thyme. Cover and simmer about 30 minutes or until meat is tender.

BEEF RAGOUT

(This recipe takes time, but is delicious! You will need a blender.)

2 lbs. beef chuck, cubed
2 tbsp. oil
1 large onion, chopped
1 cup finely chopped carrot
1 cup finely chopped celery
2 cloves garlic, minced
2 tsp. salt
1 tsp. crumbled thyme leaf
1 bay leaf
¼ tsp. pepper
2 cups dry red wine
¼ cup flour

Brown the beef cubes with 1 tbsp. oil, a few pieces at a time, in a large pot. Remove and set aside. Add more oil if needed and sauté the onion, carrot, celery and garlic. Stir in the salt, thyme, bay leaf and pepper. Return beef to the pot; add wine; bring to a boil slowly; lower heat to simmer and cover the pot. Simmer 1 ½ hours or until beef is very tender.

Remove bay leaf and discard. Remove beef with a slotted spoon and keep warm. Pour half the liquid into a blender with half the flour. Cover and mix at high speed 1 minute. Repeat with the rest of liquid and flour. Return liquid to pot and bring to a boil. Cook while stirring constantly, until thickened, about 3 minutes. Return beef to pot to heat. Serve beef and part of the sauce on a warm platter. Surround the meat with rice or your favorite vegetables. Put remaining sauce into a gravy or sauce dish.

CHICKEN AND TURKEY DISHES

LEMON BAKED CHICKEN

6 servings
3 lbs. frying chicken pieces
¼ cup melted margarine
3 tbsp. lemon juice
1 tsp. grated lemon peel
1 ½ cup corn flake crumbs
½ tsp. salt
1/8 tsp. pepper

Combine the crumbs with salt and pepper in a bowl large enough to dip the chicken pieces. Melt the margarine in another bowl and mix with the lemon juice and lemon peel. Line a baking sheet with foil.

Dip the chicken in margarine/lemon mixture and then roll in the corn flakes. Place the pieces on the baking sheet with larger pieces on the outer rim. Sprinkle any leftover cornflake crumbs over the chicken. Bake at 350⁰ about 1 hour or until chicken is tender. Do not turn the chicken.

GAYINA CON TOMAT (CHICKEN IN TOMATO SAUCE)

1 frying chicken, cut up
2 tbsp. oil
1 large can diced tomatoes, drained
1 onion, chopped (optional)
1 tsp. salt and pepper to taste
Water

Heat the oil in a large skillet or oven-proof dish. Season the chicken and brown it. Add the tomatoes and a little water. Cover and bake at 350⁰ for 40-50 minutes. Take cover off and bake 10-15 minutes more. Serve with fideos. (See Pasta and Rice section.)

ARROZ CON POLLO (CHICKEN WITH RICE)

Serves 5-6

1 frying chicken, cut up
¾ cup chopped onion
1 green pepper, chopped

1 tsp. salt

Pepper to taste

2 cloves minced garlic

½ cup oil

1 can chicken broth

3 cups canned tomatoes

1 tsp. cumin

¼ tsp. saffron

1 cup long-grain rice, washed

½ cup white wine

½ cup frozen peas (optional)

Fry the chicken until evenly browned in a large skillet or casserole dish. Remove chicken. Sauté the onions, garlic, green pepper with salt, pepper and cumin for 5 minutes. Replace chicken. Add tomatoes and peas. Add rice with broth, wine and saffron. Bring to a boil, cover and simmer 30 minutes or cook in oven at 350⁰ for 40 minutes or until liquid is absorbed and rice is fluffy. Garnish with some Spanish olives if desired.

CHICKEN CACCIATORE

1 3 lb. chicken, cut up or 8 skinless boneless chicken thighs

3 tbsp. oil

1 large onion chopped

1 green pepper chopped

¾ cup fresh white mushrooms, sliced

1 large can stewed tomatoes or 1 8 oz. can tomato sauce

½ cup red or white wine

2 cloves garlic minced

½ tsp. oregano

Salt and pepper to taste

¼ cup fresh chopped parsley, optional for garnish

Heat 2 tbsp. of the oil in a large deep skillet. Brown the chicken on all sides. Transfer chicken to a plate. Pour off fat, add a tbsp. of oil. Add the onion, garlic, green pepper, mushrooms. Sauté on medium heat until all is tender. Add the tomatoes, wine and seasoning. Bring to a simmer over moderately high heat. Reduce heat and return chicken to the skillet. Cover and cook until chicken is tender about 45 minutes. Turn the pieces occasionally. Remove cover the last 10-15 minutes if sauce is too thin. Serve over spaghetti.

ROASTED CHICKEN AND VEGETABLES

1 whole chicken

1 large onion cut in wedges

4 carrots, trimmed and halved

4 celery stalks cut in 3 inch pieces

Salt and pepper

Juice of 1 lemon

3 large baking potatoes, peeled and cut in large chunks

3 tbsp. olive oil

½ tsp. each dried thyme, rosemary, oregano and basil

Twine

Preheat oven to 375⁰. Prepare vegetables and toss with 2 tbsp. oil, salt and pepper. Line a shallow roasting pan with the vegetables. Remove giblets and neck from the chicken and discard. Rub chicken with remaining oil and spices. Splash the cavity with the lemon juice for tenderness. Tie the legs together with twine. Place chicken, breast side up, on top of vegetables and roast for 65-75 minutes until chicken is browned and vegetables are tender. Check doneness when thigh juices run clear when pierced by a fork or with a thermometer in thickest inside part of thigh. It is done at 165⁰. Let chicken rest for 10 minutes before carving. Keep vegetables warm until ready to serve.

CHICKEN IN THE POT

1 fryer chicken, cut up

1 large onion, sliced

2 tsp. salt

¼ tsp. ground pepper

¼ tsp. dried thyme

1 bay leaf

3 large carrots, peeled and cut in chunks

2 large potatoes, peeled and cut in chunks

¼ cup flour

Place chicken pieces in a 6-quart Dutch oven and cover with 2 ½ cups water. Add onion, salt, pepper, thyme, bay leaf, potatoes and carrots. Bring to a boil; reduce heat, and simmer, covered, 45 minutes or until tender. Combine the flour with ¼ cup water in a small bowl. Stir until dissolved and add to the broth in the pan to thicken it. Bring to a boil while stirring. Serves 4-6

CROCK POT CHICKEN CHILI

2 chicken breasts cut in chunks

1 can black beans

1 can of kidney beans

1 can corn

1 large can diced tomatoes

1-2 pkgs. taco seasoning

Throw everything into a crock pot and cook 4-6 hours.

CHICKEN AND NOODLES

1 package egg noodles
2 tbsp. olive oil
4 large pieces of boned chicken cut in chunks
Olive oil for frying
2 tbsp. garlic, minced
2 tbsp. Italian Seasoning
2 tbsp. parsley
Salt and pepper to taste
Parmesan Cheese or vegan cheese, such as PARMA!

Cook noodles according to package directions and stir with olive oil. Bake or sauté chicken in olive oil with garlic and seasoning until done. Add chicken to noodles and serve hot.

VARIATION: Add sautéed mushrooms or bell peppers or both.

TURKEY MEATLOAF

1 large onion, chopped
1 tbsp. olive oil
2 cloves garlic, minced
¾ tsp. salt
½ tsp. pepper
1 ½ tsp. Worcestershire sauce
1/3 cup chicken broth
1 tbsp. ketchup
1 ½ lbs. ground turkey
3/4 cup breadcrumbs or quick-cooking oats
2 large eggs or1 large egg and 1 large egg white, beaten
TOPPING:
2 tbsp. ketchup

Preheat oven to 375⁰.

Sauté the onion until it is tender. Add garlic and 1/4 tsp. each salt and pepper. Add Worcestershire sauce, broth and 1 tbsp. ketchup. Cool in a large bowl.

Next, add turkey, crumbs, and eggs with remaining salt and pepper. Mix well. Place moist mixture in a loaf pan or form a loaf and place on a foil-lined baking sheet. Top with 2 tbsp. ketchup and bake 1 hour.

Let stand a few minutes before serving.

TURKEY MEATBALLS

1 lb. ground turkey
½ cup quick-cooking oats
3-4 tbsp. chopped onion
1 egg
3 tbsp. tomato sauce
Salt and pepper to taste
1 tsp. Italian seasoning
1- 1 ½ cups tomato sauce for simmering

Mix first 7 ingredients and make 1-inch balls. Bake in a shallow pan at 400° for 20 minutes. Transfer to a pot with tomato sauce and simmer 10-15 minutes before serving.

FISH

PISHKADO CON AGRESTADA (FISH WITH LEMON-EGG SAUCE)

ALSO CALLED PISHKADO CON UEVO Y LIMÓN

2 lbs. fish, preferably salmon fillets or steaks
1 tsp. salt and a little white pepper
1 tbsp. olive or salad oil
2 tbsp. fresh lemon juice
2 eggs, beaten
2-3 tbsp. finely chopped parsley
½ cup water or more to cover fish

Cut fish into serving pieces and place in a 10-12" deep-sided frying pan, single layer. Add enough water to just cover the fish. Add salt, pepper, oil, half the parsley and 1 tbsp. lemon juice. Bring to a boil slowly to poach 5-10 minutes. The fish should just begin to flake. Transfer fish carefully to a serving dish while leaving the liquid in the pan.

SAUCE: Beat the eggs in a bowl with the rest of the lemon juice. Add a few tablespoons of poaching water slowly. Pour this egg mixture back into the pan and cook on low heat until the sauce is thickened, about 5 minutes. Shake the pan to blend sauce well. Do not boil! Add the rest of the parsley. Pour sauce over the fish. Serve immediately or, cool, and refrigerate, covered with plastic wrap to serve it cold later. Perfect for a holiday meal!

PISHKADO CON TOMAT (FISH IN TOMATO SAUCE)

1 lb. white fish or salmon fillet cut in serving pieces
1 cup tomato sauce
Juice of ½ of lemon
1 tsp. salt
2 tbsp. oil
1 tbsp. chopped parsley
Four to coat fish
¼ cup water

In a deep-sided pan place the oil. Coat the fish slices in flour and place them in the pan. Add the tomato sauce, water, lemon juice and salt. Cover and cook on medium heat for 15 minutes. Sprinkle with parsley and simmer a few minutes before serving.

VARIATIONS:

1. Boil sauce ingredients and simmer 10 minutes. Place fish in a baking pan, pour sauce over, cover and bake a half hour at 350⁰. Remove cover and broil until browned.

2. Dip fish (I like this with salmon steaks) in flour and then egg and fry in hot oil. Add the sauce, cover and simmer on stove-top or bake as above.

FRIED SMELT or TROUT

Fresh smelt
1-2 beaten eggs
Flour for coating
Salt and pepper
Oil for frying

Clean fish and season with salt and pepper. Coat fish with flour and dip in egg. Fry both sides in hot oil until golden brown. Pick a sauce for fried fish from below.

VARIATION: Use fillet of sole, tilapia, salmon or halibut.

1. **VINAGRE (VINEGAR AND TOMATO SAUCE)**

   2 cloves garlic, minced

   2 tbsp. oil

   ¼ cup tomato sauce

   3 tbsp. vinegar

   1 tsp. sugar

   1 tsp. salt

   2 tbsp. flour

   1 cup water

   1 tbsp. chopped parsley

   Heat the oil and sauté the garlic a little in a saucepan. Mix the flour, water and vinegar in a separate bowl. Add all ingredients to the garlic and bring to a boil. Reduce heat and simmer. Stir occasionally until sauce is thick. Remove from heat and add parsley. Sauce can be served hot or cold.

2. **AGRESTADA (LEMON SAUCE FOR FRIED FISH)**

   2 eggs

   Juice of 1-2 lemons

   2 tbsp. oil

   1 tsp. salt

   3 tbsp. flour

   2 cups water

   Beat the eggs. Add lemon juice, oil and salt. Mix a few tablespoons of the water with the flour to make a smooth paste and then add the rest of the water. Cook on medium heat while stirring constantly with a wooden spoon to prevent lumps. The sauce is ready when it thickens enoufh to coat the back of the spoon. Serve warm.

LEMON BROILED FISH

2 lbs. fish, salmon, tilapia, cod, your choice
Juice of 1 lemon
2 tbsp. olive oil
1 tsp. salt and pepper to taste
¼ tsp. paprika

Mix the lemon juice with oil and paprika. Coat fish and marinate a few minutes. Arrange fish on a broiler rack coated with cooking spray. Sprinkle with salt and pepper. Broil 8 minutes or until fish is easily flaked with a fork.

BUTTER WINE SAUCE (for any broiled or grilled fish)

For 1 cup
12 oz. butter, cut into ½" cubes
2 minced shallots
Grated zest of 1 lemon
1 ½ tbsp. lemon juice
¾ cup white wine
Salt to taste

In a saucepan over medium-low heat, melt 1 tbsp. butter. Add shallots and zest and sauté for 5 minutes. Add juice and wine. Reduce heat and simmer until mixture is reduced to 1/3 cup, 20 minutes. Add butter and whisk, a little at a time. Strain sauce through a sieve and add salt.

MEDITERRANEAN COD

1 lb. cod fillets
2 tbsp. olive oil
1 onion, thinly sliced
1 can (14 1/2 oz) diced tomatoes
½ cup black olives (I use kalamatas)
½ cup dry white wine
2 cloves garlic, minced
1 tbsp. parsley, chopped

Heat the oil in a large frying pan. Sauté the onions and garlic until tender. Stir in tomatoes, olives, parsley, and wine. Simmer 5 minutes. Place fillets in the sauce and simmer 5 minutes more.

Serve over pasta, rice, or quinoa, my favorite.

MEDITERRANEAN COD

TUNA CASSEROLE

2 cups cooked egg noodles or your favorite pasta
1 can of condensed cream of mushroom soup
½ cup milk
1 cup frozen peas, thawed
¼ cup onion, minced (optional)
1 can tuna (7 oz), drained
2 tbsp. melted butter
½ cup dried bread or cracker crumbs or crushed potato chips
¼ cup parmesan cheese (optional topping)

Preheat oven to 375⁰. Cook noodles according to package directions; drain and rinse. Place in a mixing bowl. Mix soup and milk together. Add to the noodles with tuna and peas. Gently stir. Melt butter in a 2-quart casserole dish. Turn bowl contents into dish. Sprinkle with topping of your choice. Bake 25 minutes or until bubbly.

KIFTES DE PESCADO (SALMON BALLS)

1 large can salmon, drained and deboned, or 1½ cups cooked salmon
2 slices bread, soaked and squeezed dry
2 tbsp. parsley, minced
1 onion, finely chopped
1 tbsp. chopped dill
3 eggs, beaten (you can substitute 1 egg with egg white)
Salt and pepper to taste
Vegetable oil for frying

Chop fish. Add remaining ingredients. Form small balls and fry in hot oil.

VARIATIONS: Use 1 cup mashed potatoes instead of bread. For croquettes, make balls with just 1 egg. Dip balls in a bowl with 2 beaten eggs and then, dip in a bowl of 2-1 bread crumbs and flour mixture. Deep fry the balls 4 at a time in 3-4 inches hot oil.

OVEN-FRIED FISH AND CHIPS

THE FISH

1 ½ lb. skinless cod fillet or fillet of your choice
1 ½ cups bread crumbs
½ tsp. dry dill weed, dry basil or dry Italian herbs or 1 tsp. Old Bay seasoning
3 tbsp. vegetable oil

Preheat oven to 400⁰. Place crumbs in a plate. Mix with the seasoning of your choice. Rinse fish and pat dry. Cut crosswise in 2-inch strips. Pour oil in another plate. Roll fish in oil. Let excess drip off before coating fish all over in crumbs. Arrange strips of fish on a baking sheet 1 inch apart. Bake until fish is opaque or flaky 8-10 minutes.

THE FRIES

2 large baking potatoes
1 tbsp. olive oil
2 tsp. dried thyme
1 tbsp. garlic powder
2 tsp. cornstarch
1-2 tsp. Kosher salt

Preheat oven to 450⁰. Line a baking sheet with foil and heat it on a lower rack.

Slice potatoes into ¼-inch rounds and toss with olive oil. Mix remaining ingredients together and toss with the potatoes. Place on the hot baking sheet and cook 25-30 minutes on the lower rack of oven. Half way through cooking, turn the potato slices.

PAN-FRIED SALMON

½ whole salmon fillet cut into serving pieces
1 cup flour
Salt and pepper to taste
1 tbsp. seafood seasoning (I like Johnny's)
3-4 tbsp. butter or margarine

Heat a skillet with butter or margarine. Place flour and seasonings in a paper sack and shake. Take one serving piece of salmon and place in bag. Shake until well coated. Place fish, flesh side down, in skillet. Repeat with more pieces of fish. Fry 5-7 minutes and turn the fish to fry a few minutes more. Make sure flesh is flaky. Serve immediately.

TERIYAKI SALMON

Cooking oil spray
2 tbsp. water
¼ cup light brown sugar, packed
2 tbsp. rice vinegar
2 tbsp. reduced sodium soy sauce
½ tsp. ground ginger
½ tsp. garlic powder
4 salmon fillets
Chopped scallions for garnish (optional)

Preheat oven to 400⁰. Spray oil over a shallow roasting pan.

In a shallow dish, whisk water, sugar, vinegar, soy sauce, ginger and garlic. Coat salmon fillets in the mixture. Optionally, marinate, covered, in the refrigerator up to 1 hour. Place salmon on roasting pan and pour excess sauce over it. Roast 15 minutes or until flaky with a fork. Serve over your favorite noodles. Spoon teriyaki sauce left in pan over the salmon and sprinkle with scallions.

SOLE AMANDINE

½ cup sliced almonds
1/3 cup butter or margarine
1 tbsp. grated lemon peel
Salt and pepper to taste
½ tsp. dill weed
1 lb. fresh sole fillets or frozen sole, thawed and drained

Heat the oven to 350⁰. Spread almonds over a 13x9" baking pan. Add butter and bake for about 7 minutes until butter is melted. Stir and continue baking for 4 minutes or until almonds are lightly- toasted. Stir in lemon peel, dill weed, salt and pepper. Dip the fillets into the almond / butter mixture, coating both sides. Scoop up remaining almonds with a spoon and spread over fillets. Continue baking 15 to 20 minutes or until the fish flakes with a fork.

SEPHARDIC VEGGIES and BEANS

FASULIA (STRING BEANS IN TOMATO SAUCE)

2 lbs. fresh green beans or whole frozen cut in halves
1 onion, diced
1 can (14 1/2 oz.) diced tomatoes or 3-4 fresh, peeled and diced
1 tsp. salt
1 tbsp. oil
1 cup water
1 tbsp. lemon juice, optional
½ tsp. sugar, optional

Clean and string the beans with a potato peeler. Cut in halves. No need to string frozen beans. Sauté the onion. Add the tomatoes, salt, lemon and water. Bring to a boil. Add the green beans. Cover and cook on low heat for 45 minutes or until beans are tender.

FASULIA

BERENGENA FRITA (FRIED EGGPLANT)

1 large eggplant
½ tsp. salt and water for soaking
½ cup flour (mix with1/4 cup matzo meal or bread crumbs for crunchiness, optional)
Salt and pepper to taste
1-2 beaten eggs
Oil for frying

Peel and slice eggplant across in ½ inch rounds. Soak in salted water a few minutes. Drain. Add salt and pepper to flour. Dip the slices into flour and beaten egg. Brown both sides 2-3 minutes each in hot oil. Drain on paper towels.

VARIATION:

1. Sprinkle slices with Parmesan or Romano Cheese.

2. Make a sauce of ½ cup tomato sauce, ½ cup water, 1 clove garlic, sautéed and ½ tsp. sugar. Place slices in sauce and simmer 30 minutes.

EGGPLANT IN TOMATO SAUCE

1 large eggplant
1 large onion
1 bell pepper, sliced
2-3 tbsp. oil
½ cup tomato sauce
½ tsp. salt
1 tsp. sugar
¼ tsp. pepper
1 cup water

Peel and slice the eggplant across in ½ inch rounds. Soak in salted water a few minutes. Meanwhile, in a large saucepan, sauté the onion and pepper slices in oil. Drain the eggplant slices and place over the onions. Mix the remaining ingredients and pour over the eggplant. Cover and bring to a boil. Reduce heat and simmer about a 30 minutes until most of the liquid has evaporated.

BAMIA (OKRA IN TOMATO SAUCE)

(I hated this dish when my mother used to make it. I grew to love it in adulthood, especially with rice)

1 pkg. frozen okra
1/2 cup tomato sauce
Juice of 1 lemon
1-2 cloves garlic, minced
1 onion, chopped
Salt and pepper to taste
½ cup water
2 tbsp. oil

Partially thaw the okra. Sauté the onion. Add the okra and cover with tomato sauce. Add rest of ingredients. Bring to a boil. Cover and simmer for 30-40 minutes. Serve hot or cold as a side dish or as an appetizer.

CARNABEET FRITA (FRIED CAULIFLOWER)

1 fresh cauliflower, whole or precut in a package
1 beaten egg
½ cup flour
Salt to taste
Oil for frying

Clean and trim cauliflower. Place in boiling salted water for a few minutes or skip this step if you like crunchiness. Drain and cut into flowerets. (I often cut large flowerets in half for easy frying) Dip into flour and then egg. Brown the flowerets in oil to desired taste. Season and drain on paper towels.

CUALIFLOWER MEDELY

Follow directions above for fried cauliflower

1 large potato, cut up
3 ribs celery, chopped
3 tbsp. tomato sauce
1 cup water
Juice of 1 lemon
Salt to taste

Cook potato and celery with tomato sauce and water for 15 minutes. Use an oven-proof pan or casserole dish. Add the cauliflower, salt and lemon juice. Cover and bake for 30 minutes in a 350⁰ oven.

AVICAS (BEANS)

2 cans (15oz) Great Northern beans or white navy beans, drained and rinsed
2 onions, chopped
½ cup tomato sauce or 2 tomatoes, diced
¼ cup oil
Salt and pepper to taste
3 cups water or vegetable broth

Sauté the onions. Add the rest of the ingredients and bring to a boil. Lower heat and simmer 15 minutes. Serve with rice.

VARIATION: Sauté some lamb ribs or stew meat with the onions.

SPINACH AND BEANS

1 bunch fresh cleaned spinach or 1 package frozen
1 onion, chopped
2 tbsp. oil
1 can Great Northern or garbanzo beans, rinsed
¼ cup tomato sauce
Juice of ½ lemon
1 tsp. salt
½ cup water or broth for frozen spinach, 1 cup for fresh

Sauté the onion. Add frozen spinach that has been broken up or fresh spinach with the remaining ingredients. Bring to a boil. Cover and simmer about a 10 minutes.

SPINACH AND RICE

2 bunches fresh spinach, cleaned and cut, including stems
2 tbsp. oil
½ cup rice
½ cup water
1 tsp. salt
Juice of 1 lemon or more to taste

Place all ingredients in a large saucepan. Cook on medium heat 30 minutes, or until rice is done.

KASHKARICAS (ZUCCHINI PEEL)

(This one is great for you gardeners growing large zucchinis!)

Thick outer skin of 2 very large zucchini (about 5 cups)
1 cup water
2 tbsp. lemon juice
2 tbsp. oil
1 tsp. salt
2 tsp. sugar
1 clove garlic, minced

Place all in a saucepan and cook over medium heat for 40-50 minutes until peels are tender.

4 servings

FIJONES (BLACK-EYED PEAS)

1 onion, chopped
1 tbsp. oil
2 cans black-eyed peas or frozen equivalent
1 tomato peeled and chopped, or ¼ cup tomato sauce

1 cup water
1 tsp. salt

Sauté the onion and tomato in a saucepan . Add the other ingredients. Bring to a boil, cover and simmer about 10 minutes. Add more water or chicken broth as needed.

POTATOES AND CELERY

4 stalks celery
3 potatoes
2 cups broth, your choice
2 tbsp. oil
¼ cup lemon juice, optional

Clean and string celery and then cut into small pieces. Cook the celery with the broth, salt and oil for 30 minutes or until celery in tender. Peel and cut potatoes in chunks. Add the potatoes and simmer until done.

VARIATION: Add 1 cup diced tomatoes.

CALABASA (STEWED ZUCCHINI)

6 medium zucchini squash
1 onion, chopped
1 tomato, peeled and chopped or ½ can diced tomatoes
1 clove garlic, minced
1 tbsp. olive oil
1 tsp. sugar
1-2 tbsp. chopped parsley
½ tsp. salt
Pepper to taste

Peel zucchini if you wish and cut into large rounds. Add remaining ingredients and simmer for 15 minutes on low heat.

OTHER VEGETABLES & POTATOES

MAPLE-GLAZED CARROTS

3 ½ cups baby carrots
1 tbsp. butter, melted
2 tsp. pure maple syrup
Sea salt and pepper to taste
Pinch of cinnamon and nutmeg

Steam carrots over boiling water until tender (5-10 minutes). Use a pot with a steamer basket. Pour butter and syrup in a sauté pan. Drain carrots and sauté a few minutes in the syrup and butter over medium-high heat.

ROASTED BABY CARROTS

Cooking spray
3 pkgs. (16 oz) baby carrots
Olive oil to drizzle
Garlic salt to taste

Preheat oven to 300°. Coat a large oven casserole dish with cooking spray. Spread out carrots evenly in the dish. Drizzle with olive oil and garlic salt. Roast for 60-80 minutes or until carrots become soft and turn golden brown. Stir carrots every 15 minutes and drizzle on more oil if needed.

ROASTED ASPARAGUS

1-2 lbs. fresh asparagus washed and trimmed. (Trim by snapping off hard ends)
½ tsp. salt
½ tsp. garlic powder
Olive oil for drizzling
Lemon wedges for garnish, optional

Preheat oven to 350°. Spray or drizzle olive oil on a large baking pan. Place asparagus spears single file, not overlapping on the pan. Drizzle with more olive oil. Sprinkle with salt and garlic powder. Roll the spears to make sure they are coated. Roast for 20 minutes.

SKILLET ASPARAGUS

1 ½ lbs asparagus
2 tbsp. butter or margarine
2 tsp. lemon juice
½ tsp. salt

Wash and trim asparagus by bending off the ends where stalks are tough. In a large skillet, melt the butter on medium heat. Add the asparagus, lemon juice and salt. Cover and cook about 5 minutes until asparagus is tender but crisp. Turn occasionally. 6-8 servings

BAKED EGGPLANT with CHEESE

1 medium eggplant
1/4 cup melted margarine or olive oil
½ cup tomato or spaghetti sauce
4 oz. mozzarella
½ cup Parmesan
1 tbsp. dried basil

Slice unpeeled eggplant crosswise ½" thick. Brush slices with margarine, coating both sides. Broil until golden brown. Place in single layer in a shallow baking pan. Spread on tomato sauce and sprinkle with the cheeses. Bake at 350^0 just until cheese melts. Top with basil.

STEAMED BROCCOLI WITH HOLLANDAISE SAUCE

2 stalks broccoli
1 inch of boiling water in bottom of a saucepan
½ tsp. salt

Wash broccoli several times. Remove outer leaves. Trim off lower ends of stalk. On a cutting board, cut stalks in half length wise and place in a shallow wide bottom pan. Sprinkle with salt. Pour over boiling water to ½ inch. Cover, bring to a boil, reduce heat and cook at boiling point 8-10 minutes. Place in a shallow serving dish. Pour over ready-made or packaged Hollandaise sauce or make your own as follows:

SAUCE:

1 ½ tbsp. lemon juice
¾ cup butter
3 egg yolks, well beaten
Dash of salt

Divide butter into 3 pieces. Put I piece in top of a double boiler: add lemon juice and eggs. Place over hot water to cook slowly, beating constantly.

PARMESAN BROCCOLI

6 cups broccoli florets
3-4 tbsp. grated, fresh Parmesan cheese
½ tsp. salt

Steam broccoli florets, covered, 6 minutes or until tender and crisp. Remove from heat and toss gently with salt and cheese.

GARLIC-MASHED CAULIFLOWER

2 medium heads of cauliflower, cut into florets or small pieces
Water to boil
4 cloves garlic, minced
1 tsp. snipped fresh or dried chives
Salt and pepper to taste
¼ cup low-fat or soy sour cream
Optional toppings: unsalted butter or margarine, more chives, parmesan cheese

In a large saucepan, bring water to boil and cook cauliflower about 7 minutes or until fork tender. Drain and transfer to a large food processor. Puree with the cream cheese, garlic, salt and pepper to desired consistency. Add some water if needed. Serve with desired garnishes.

PORTOBELLO PIZZA

4 Portobello mushroom caps
2 tsp. olive oil
1 tsp. garlic powder
¾ cup marinara or pizza sauce
¾ cup shredded part-skim mozzarella cheese
Dried basil or Italian Seasoning

Preheat oven to 425⁰. Wash caps. Rub oil all over and sprinkle gills with garlic powder. Place mushroom caps on a baking sheet gill side down. Roast 20 minutes. Turn the caps over and top each with marinara sauce and cheese. Sprinkle basil over all. Bake until the cheese melts and mushrooms are tender, 2-3 minutes.

FETA-STUFFED TOMATOES

4 plum tomatoes cut in half
Olive oil spray
2 tbsp. dry breadcrumbs
3 tbsp. crumbled feta cheese
¼ tsp. dried basil
¼ tsp. dried oregano
Pepper to taste

Preheat oven to 350°. Put tomato halves on a baking sheet sprayed with oil. Sprinkle breadcrumbs over each half and top with cheese. Sprinkle with basil, oregano and pepper. Bake for 25 minutes.

FRIED GREEN TOMATOES

(for you gardeners)

8 ½" tomato slices
½ tsp. salt
½ cup cornmeal
1 tbsp. canola oil
½ tsp. salt and ¼ tsp. pepper
Season and dredge both sides of tomato slices in cornmeal. Fry each side about 3 minutes. Drain on paper towels.

ROASTED BUTTERNUT SQUASH

6 cups prepackaged peeled and cubed butternut squash
2 tbsp. olive oil
1 tsp. cumin
1 tsp. salt
½ tsp. allspice
Pepper to taste

Preheat oven to 425°. Place squash in a large bowl and toss with oil. Combine the spices and sprinkle on the squash, coating evenly. Lay squash in a single layer on a large baking sheet and roast 40 minutes. Turn squash often.

ACORN SQUASH WITH HONEY

3 medium acorn squash
¼ cup butter or margarine, melted
¼ tsp. cinnamon
½ tsp. salt
1/3 cup honey

Preheat oven to375°. Wash squash and cut in half lengthwise. Remove seeds and fibers. Arrange squash, cut side down, in a shallow baking pan. Surround them with ½ inch of hot water. Bake 30 minutes. Combine remaining ingredients in a small bowl. Pour off excess liquid from baking pan. Turn squash cut side up. Pour sauce from bowl into cavities and bake 15 minutes, basting occasionally with the sauce.

SQUASH AND APPLES

2 acorn butternut squash
Salt to taste
2 medium apples, peeled and sliced
8 tbsp. brown sugar
4 tbsp. butter or margarine

Cinnamon to sprinkle

Cut squash in half and remove seeds. Place cut-side down in a shallow baking dish. Bake at 375°25-30 minutes. With cut-side up, sprinkle with salt. Fill cavities with apples and top each with 2 tbsp. brown sugar, 1 tbsp. butter and a sprinkling of cinnamon. Cook 15-20 minutes or until all is tender.

RATATOUILLE (A FRENCH VEGETABLE MEDLEY)

1 medium yellow onion chopped in chunks
2 cloves garlic, minced
4 tbsp. olive oil
3 Roma tomatoes cut into wedges
1 medium eggplant cut into 1x2" strips
2 zucchini cut into ½' slices
1 green pepper seeded and cut into strips
1 tsp. dried basil
1/.2 tsp. dried thyme
1 tbsp. chopped parsley
Salt and pepper to taste
Gruyere or mozzarella topping, optional

Sprinkle eggplant and zucchini with salt and let stand 30 minutes. Drain, rinse and dry on paper towels. Sauté the onions in 2 tablespoons oil in a large pan until tender. Layer the onions, eggplant, zucchini, green pepper and tomatoes. Combine the garlic and seasonings minus the parsley and sprinkle over the vegetables. Mix all well. Add the remaining oil on top. Cover and simmer over medium heat about 30 minutes until the vegetables are softened. Do not overcook! Stir in parsley just before serving.

SCALLOPED CORN

1 16 oz can creamed corn
¼ cup chopped onion
1 egg slightly beaten
1/3 cup milk
2 tbsp. butter or margarine, melted
1 cup or more crumbled saltine crackers
½ cup crushed Ritz crackers for topping

Combine first 5 ingredients in a medium bowl. Add saltines (more if mixture is soupy). Pour mixture into a casserole dish and top with Ritz crackers. Bake in 350° oven for 30-35 minutes.

ROASTED BEETS

6-8 beets or more
Olive oil
Salt and fresh ground pepper

Preheat oven to 375⁰. Rinse and trim beets. Wrap them in heavy aluminum foil. Roast 1- 1½ hours. Remove from oven and cool. Peel beets using a paring knife or by just pushing the skins. Slice, place in a bowl and drizzle with olive oil, salt and pepper.

SEASONED OVEN FRIES

3-4 medium potatoes, unpeeled
1 tbsp. lemon juice
2 tsp. olive oil
1 tsp. dried oregano
Salt and pepper to taste
2 cloves garlic, minced
Cooking spray

Cut potatoes lengthwise into 8 wedges. Mix the next 5 ingredients in a large bowl. Toss the potatoes in the mixture. Put potatoes, skin side down, on a baking sheet sprayed with oil. Bake at 400⁰ about 45 minutes until potatoes are lightly browned.

ROASTED NEW POTATOES

10-12 red new potatoes, scrubbed and cut in half
½ cup melted butter
½ cup fresh chopped parsley, divided
Salt and pepper to taste
Cooking oil spray

Coat a baking sheet with spray oil. Combine melted butter, ½ parsley, salt and pepper in a large bowl. Coat the potatoes in the bowl and spread them onto the baking sheet. Roast at 400⁰ for 30-40 minutes until slightly browned. Turn potatoes occasionally. Garnish with the rest of the parsley.

GARLIC MASHED POTATOES

5 large potatoes, washed, peeled and cut into I" pieces
3 cloves garlic, chopped
3 cups chicken broth
1 tbsp. chopped chives
Salt and pepper to taste

Combine potatoes, garlic and broth and bring to a boil. Reduce heat and simmer 10-15 minutes. Drain and reserve liquid. Mash potatoes, adding as much reserved liquid to get desired consistency.

SOUR CREAM MASHED POTATOES

2 lbs. potatoes, peeled and cut into 2" cubes
2 tbsp. butter or margarine
1 cup low-fat sour cream

Salt and pepper to taste

Garnish of chopped chives

Preheat oven to 350⁰. Butter a 2-quart baking dish. In a large saucepan, cover potatoes with cold, salted water. Bring to a boil; partially cover, and cook for 20 minutes until tender. Drain potatoes and mash them in the pot with a masher. Turn on the heat and whisk in the butter and sour cream. Add salt and pepper. Place potatoes in the baking dish and bake for 15 minutes. Garnish with chives.

BAKED PO TATOES WITH BROCCOLI

4 russet potatoes

1 small head broccoli cut in florets or 1 10 oz. pkg. frozen, chopped, thawed and drained

2 tbsp. butter or margarine

1 small onion, chopped fine

½ cup ranch dressing

1 tbsp. vegetable oil spray

Salt and pepper

1 tbsp. diced parsley

Prick potatoes several times with a fork. Microwave them on high about 15 minutes until tender. Set aside. Slice off potato tops. Scoop out all pulp while keeping skins intact. Discard tops. Mash pulp in a bowl. Heat a small skillet. Add butter and sauté onion a few minutes. Add the onion, broccoli and ranch dressing to pulp. Mix well. Spray outer potato skins with oil. Spoon the mixture into shells evenly. Place potatoes on a baking sheet and bake at 425⁰ for 15 minutes. Sprinkle with salt, pepper and parsley.

SLICED BAKED POTATOES

4 medium potatoes

1 tsp. salt

1/8 tsp. pepper

3 tbsp. melted butter or margarine

3 tbsp. dried parsley and chives or fresh, chopped

2 tbsp. Parmesan cheese, optional

Peel potatoes and cut into thin slices crosswise, but not all the way through. Place potatoes in a baking dish and dry them a bit. Sprinkle with salt and drizzle with butter and herbs. Bake at 425⁰ for 1 hour. Remove from oven and sprinkle with pepper and cheese, if desired.

FANCY POTATOES ANNA

3-4 medium russet potatoes, peeled

5 tbsp. unsalted butter, melted

2 tbsp. vegetable oil

Salt and white pepper to taste

1/8 tsp. nutmeg

Preheat oven to 400º. Slice potatoes 1/8inch thick. Use a mandolin slicer, if you have one. Dry lightly with a towel to hold in the starch. Heat the oil and 2 tablespoons butter in a 7 or 8 inch nonstick skillet with an ovenproof handle. Don't let butter brown. Remove from heat. Arrange a layer of potato slices overlapping in a spiral in the bottom of the pan. The design will appear on top when inverted. Add another layer of potatoes. They need not form a design. Sprinkle with seasoning and butter. Repeat until all potatoes are used.

Cook over medium heat 10-15 minutes until potatoes are browned on the bottom. Test by sliding a spatula down the side of potatoes and lift a little. For a crisp bottom, leave uncovered; for a softer cake, cover with f. Place skillet in the center of oven and cook 25-30 minutes, pressing potatoes occasionally with a spatula until tender. Test with a skewer. Shake the pan occasionally to keep from sticking.

To serve, loosen edges with a spatula. Place a flat platter over potatoes. Hold it firmly and invert so potatoes fall onto platter.

NOTE: The potatoes can be made 6-8 hours ahead. Keep them covered at room temperature and reheat over low heat.

ROASTED FINGERLING POTATOES

2 lbs. fingerling potatoes, halved
¼ cup olive oil
2 cloves garlic, minced
1 tbsp. rosemary
1 tsp. onion powder
½ tsp. salt
¼ tsp. pepper

Preheat oven to 425º. In a large bowl, combine potatoes and the rest of the ingredients. Toss to coat all the potatoes. Spread potatoes on a rimmed baking. Roast potatoes 30-40 minutes until tender, stirring them with a spatula halfway through.

POTATO-SPINACH PUFFS

2 ½ c ups mashed potatoes
1 ½ cups raw spinach, chopped
4 tbsp. butter or margarine, melted
1 tsp. salt
Dash each of pepper and paprika
4 eggs, separated

Combine everything except eggs. Blend in 4 egg yolks. Beat 4 whites until stiff and fold into mixture. Pile lightly into a 1 ½ quart greased casserole dish. Bake at 375º until puffed and golden, about 40 minutes. (Makes six servings)

STEAMED ZUCCHINI

4-6 zucchini, trimmed and cut into rounds, <u>not</u> peeled
Butter or margarine to taste
Mrs. Dash Seasoning or some other brand

Place zucchini rounds in a pan with just a little water. Bring to a boil. Reducer heart and cover tightly. Cook for 5-7 minutes until tender. Drain, add butter and seasoning and toss lightly.

GARLIC ZUCCHINI

4 cups chopped zucchini
3 garlic cloves, minced
¼ tsp. salt and pepper
1 tsp. olive oil
2 tbsp. Parmesan cheese

Heat the oil on medium-high. Add zucchini, garlic, salt and pepper. Sauté 4 minutes, or until tender. Sprinkle on cheese.

BEAN DISHES

GREEK CANNELINI BEANS

2 large cans cannellini beans
1 small can tomato sauce
1 medium onion, sliced thin
2 tbsp. olive oil
½ tsp. oregano
½ cup water
Salt and pepper to taste

Preheat oven to 350⁰. Mix all the ingredients and place in a 9x13" casserole. Bake for an hour.

STEAMED SUGAR-SNAP PEAS

2 tsp. olive oil
1 tbsp. water
1 lb. sugar-snap peas, ends trimmed and stringed
3 green onions, sliced
1-2 tsp. soy sauce
1 ½ tsp. raw honey
Salt and pepper to taste

Heat oil and water in a pan with a lid over medium heat. Add the peas, onions, soy sauce and honey. Cover and cook 5-7 minutes until tender. Season and serve warm.

LENTILS

½ cup onion, chopped fine
1 cup shredded carrot
2 tbsp. olive oil
2 cloves garlic, minced
¼ tsp. cumin
2/3 cup dried lentils
1 1/3 cups chicken or vegetable broth
1 1/3 cup water
Salt and pepper to taste

Over medium-high heat, cook onion and carrots in the oil for about 5 minutes. Add the rest of the ingredients and bring to a boil. Reduce heat, cover and simmer 10-15 minutes, or until all the liquid is absorbed.

QUICK REFRIED BEANS

6 tbsp. margarine or butter
2 cans kidney or pinto beans, drained and rinsed
1 tsp. salt
1/8 tsp. chili powder
1/8 tsp. cumin

Melt margarine in a large, heavy skillet. Add beans and mash with a potato masher. Stir in season ing and cook over low heat until thick and bubbling. Stir often.

BLACK BEAN TACOS

1 onion, chopped fine
1 bell pepper, chopped fine
1 tbsp. olive oil
2 cloves garlic, minced'
3 cups rinsed and drained black beans
1 cup salsa
1 cup shredded cheddar cheese
2-3 cups shredded lettuce
12 (6-inch) corn tortillas

Heat the oil in a large skillet over medium-high heat. Add the onion and peppers. Cook until golden brown. Add the garlic and cumin and cook a minute longer. Reduce heat to medium and add the beans and cook until heated, about 3 minutes.

Heat a large non-stick skillet over medium heat. Add tortillas and cook 1 minute on each side. Keep warm until ready to fill. Divide the bean mixture among the tortillas. Top each with cheese, lettuce and salsa.

EDAMAME BEANS WITH COUSCOUS

1 cup edamame, shelled, (fresh or frozen, thawed)
½ tsp. salt
¾ cup raw couscous
2 tbsp. fresh parsley, minced
1 tbsp. lemon juice
Pepper to taste

Bring 1 cup of water and salt to boil in a saucepan. Add the edamame and cook just ½ minute. Stir in the couscous, parsley and lemon juice. Remove from heat, cover tightly and let stand for 5 minutes.

ROASTED GREEN BEANS

1 tsp. each olive oil and balsamic vinegar
½ tsp. tarragon
½ tsp. salt
1 lb. green beans, washed and trimmed

Preheat oven to 500^0. Combine oil, vinegar, tarragon and salt in a large bowl. Add beans and toss to coat. Put green beans in a 13x9" baking dish. Bake for 10 minutes or until tender, but crisp.

TRADITIONAL SWEETS

BISCOCHOS (EGG SUGAR COOKIES)

(Recipe for about 4 dozen cookies)

3 eggs
¾ cup sugar
1 tsp. vanilla
A little less than ½ cup of oil
2 tsp. baking powder
3-3 ½ cups flour
Topping: 1 beaten egg and sesame seeds
Variation topping: 1 beaten egg and1/4 cup sugar mixed with ½ tsp. cinnamon

Mix eggs, oil, vanilla and sugar together. Start adding the flour mixed with baking powder, slowly, until dough is no longer sticky. Keep some extra flour on your rolling board to add if dough is too soft.. Take half of the dough and cover the rest. Roll dough to 1½ inches in diameter. Cut into 1 inch sections. (Or you can just form walnut-sized balls)

Roll pieces of dough into a rope about 6 inches long and ½ inch thick. With a knife, cut one edge with diagonal ½ inch slits (11 or 12, depending on size of cookie desired). Make a circle by joining the two ends. Place cookies on a baking sheet lined with parchment paper or sprayed lightly with oil. Brush on beaten egg and sprinkle on sesame seeds or cinnamon –sugar. (You can also pick up the cookie and dip into the topping after brushing with egg. I prefer not to handle the cookie again and to use less sesame seeds.) Bake in a preheated oven at 350⁰ for 20-25 minutes.

NOTE: If you like crispier cookies, turn oven off and let cookies sit another 10 minutes. Store cookies in covered containers or freeze.

BISCOCHOS

GLUTEN-FREE BISCOCHOS

Follow the above instructions substituting packaged gluten-free flour containing xanthan gum and doubling the amount of baking powder.

TIP: If a gluten-free recipe call for baking powder, double it.

RACHEL'S BAKLAVA (A GREEK HONEY, NUT AND FILLO CONFECTION)

Dough:

1 lb. prepared fillo dough sheets

Fillo is paperthin dough found in an oblong box (brand names of Athens or Apollo) in the frozen pastry section of a store. Costco does not carry it, but Cash and Carry and most grocery stores do.

Defrost dough by leaving it in the refrigerator overnight and letting it reach room temperature by setting the unopened box on your counter for an hour.

½-1 cup of vegetable oil for brushing fillo leaves (I choose not to use melted butter) or vegetable spray

Prepare Filling:

2 cups walnut or pecans (pecans are cheaper)

2 cups almonds (slivered almonds are easier to grind)

1/3 cup toasted sesame seeds. Optional

1 1/2 tsp. cinnamon

1/4 tsp. ground cloves

1/4 cup sugar

Grind or chop all filling ingredients together. (I chop the nuts in my blender half at a time)

Assemble Baklava:

1. Place oil in a bowl and get out a basting brush or use spray oil.. Oil the bottom and sides of a 13x9" pan.
2. Take dough out of box and lay on a flat surface, covered with plastic wrap and a damp cloth on top. Do not leave fillo uncovered for more than a couple of minutes, or it will dry out. Cut leaves to fit the bottom of your pan. Pile leaves on top of each other and keep covered until ready to use.
3. Begin by laying 5 sheets of fillo, each brushed or sprayed with oil, on the bottom of your pan. Always brush edges first to prevent crackling. Sprinkle some nut mixture evenly over the dough. Add 2 more oiled sheets of fillo and sprinkle on more nuts. Repeat until all nuts are used and pan is almost filled.

    Top with 4-5 more oiled sheets. Be sure to oil the top sheet.
4. Take a very sharp knife and cut or score through top layers of the baklava before baking. For a traditional diamond shape, cut lengthwise 1 ½" wide and another cut to make a diamond. Otherwise cut the baklava in squares which fits nicely in a paper cup to serve or, in my case, to sell.

5. Bake in a preheated oven at 350⁰ for 30-40 minutes or until golden brown. Cool slightly before cutting through remaining layers and pouring on syrup. If you are using a Teflon-coated pan, be sure not to scratch the bottom. The number of pieces will depend on the cut, about 24 diamond-shaped.

Prepare syrup:

Use equal amounts of sugar and water according to taste. I don't like oversweet baklava.
1 cup sugar
1 cup water
½ cup honey
½ tsp. lemon juice

Combine sugar and water and boil 10 -15 minutes until thickened. Add the honey and bring to a boil.

Add lemon juice. Pour evenly over pastry. Tilt the pan. Allow baklava to cool completely, perhaps overnight. Cut and remove from pan to serve or store in air-tight containers or freeze in plastic containers for up to 6 months.

MAKING BAKLAVA

BAKLAVA

BAKLAVA ROLLS

Follow above directions for handling 1 lb. of fillo, preparing the nut filling and syrup.

Layer 4 fillo sheets that have been brushed or sprayed with oil on a flat surface, long side facing you. Cut into 4 strips for small rolls. Place filling at one end of strip, leaving 1" from end and ½" from each side free. Start rolling from the edge with filling. Once the filling is covered, fold over the sides and continue rolling tightly to the end of the strip. Brush the outside and place, seam-side down, on an ungreased baking sheet 1"apart. Bake in preheated 350⁰ oven for 15-20 minutes or until golden brown. Pour syrup on individual rolls.

CURABIE (pronounced courahbeeyay) ALMOND SAND COOKIES

1 cup ground slivered almonds (grind them yourself or purchase almond meal)
½ tsp. baking soda
1 cup sugar
½ tsp. cinnamon
1 cup oil
2 ½-3 cups flour

For rolling: powdered sugar or a mixture of ½ cup sugar and ½ tsp. cinnamon.

Preheat oven to 300°. Mix sugar, oil, soda and cinnamon together. Add nuts. Gradually add enough flour to keep mixture together. Knead and shape into 1 ½" rounds. Place on an ungreased baking sheet 1" apart and bake for 30 minutes or until slightly brown. Dust or roll cookies with sugar of your choice.

TRAVADOS (HONEY ALMOND TURNOVERS)

Filling: Mix together:
3 cups ground almonds
3 tbsp. honey
1/3 cup sugar
1 tsp. cinnamon
½ tsp. ground cloves
1/3 cup water

Dough:

1 cup oil
1 egg
½ cup sugar
½ cup water
½ tsp. baking soda
4 ½-5 cups flour

Mix first 4 ingredients together. Sift flour and baking soda together and add enough to form a soft dough. Divide dough into walnut-sized pieces. Flatten by hand into circles 2 ½"-3'in diameter. Put 1 teaspoon of filling in the center, fold over, and press edges together. Decorate edges with the tines of a fork. Arrange on a baking sheet and bake in a 350° oven for 30-35 minutes until golden brown. Store in air-tight containers for a week or freeze.

Syrup: (optional)

Make syrup when ready to serve the pastry.
1 cup sugar
½ cup water
3 tbsp. honey
Boil together until sticky. Drop travados into the syrup and place on a plate to cool.

EASY MARZIPAN

2 cups almond flour or almond meal, such as Red Mill
2 cups powdered sugar
2 egg whites
Traditional decoration (optional): silver balls (dragees)

Combine almonds flour and sugar in a bowl and blend well together. Place egg whites into a cup and add a little at a time until the dough pulls away from the sides of the bowl and forms a ball. You might not use all the egg whites. Divide the dough into 5-6 balls. Roll with your hands into ropes 1" in diameter. Dip a knife into hot water to easily cut the ropes on a diagonal, forming diamond shapes. Decorate as you wish. (I sometimes decorate with sprinkles.) Freeze on a baking sheet lined with parchment paper. Later, take out of baking sheet and serve on a platter or place frozen marzipan in air-tight containers to store in the freezer and serve later.

MARZIPAN

CHANUKA BURMUELOS (TURKISH RAISED DOUGHNUTS)

Makes 25-30

3 tsp. dried yeast
½ tsp. sugar
2¼ cup warm water
¼ tsp. salt
2 cups flour
1 tbsp. vegetable oil
Oil for frying
Syrup: ¾ cup honey with 3 tbsp. water

Dissolve yeast and sugar in ½ cup of the warm water. Let rest until bubbles appear on the surface. In a large bowl, mix the yeast mixture with the rest of the warm water. Add the salt, oil and flour. Dough should be smooth. Cover and set in a warm place to rise to double in size, an hour or so. Punch down, cover again and let rise another ½ hour.

Heat 4 inches of oil to 375⁰ in a deep fryer or heavy sauce pan. Oil is hot enough when a drop of water sizzles in the oil. Prepare a small bowl of water to moisten your hands. Dip hands into the water, shaking off any excess, and grab a round piece of dough 2" in diameter. Work the dough into a ball: then stretch it to 4" while poking a hole in the middle with your finger. Try to maintain a doughnut shape. Carefully drop into the oil. Repeat 2-3 times. Avoid frying too many at one time. Cook one side until golden brown, turn and cook the other side. Remove with a slotted spoon and drain on paper towels. Repeat procedure until all the dough is used.

Heat the honey and water until hot and well mixed. Drizzle over doughnuts.

VARIATION: Serve with powdered sugar and cinnamon

NOTE: Burmuelos do not freeze well, but they can be stored in a plastic bag or container, without syrup, for a few days. Reheat in oven or about 15 seconds in a microwave oven.

CHANUKA FRITTERS

1 egg
1 cup milk
1½ cups flour
1 tsp. baking powder
Oil for frying
Syrup:
½ cup sugar
½ cup honey
1 cup water

Beat the egg and add milk. Beat thoroughly. Mix flour and baking powder together. Gradually add this mixture to egg mixture. Heat 3" of oil in a heavy 2 quart pan. Wait for oil to get very hot. Drop the batter by tablespoons. Remove with slotted spoon when golden brown. Drain on paper towels. Drizzle with syrup.

HAMENTASHEN (a filled cookie traditionally made for the Jewish festival of Purim)

DOUGH (for 4 dozen)
½ cup margarine
½ cup sugar
1½ cups flour
1 ¼ tsp. baking powder
Pinch of salt
1 tbsp. orange juice
1 egg
1 tsp. vanilla

Cream the margarine and sugar. Sift the dry ingredients and add to first mixture. Add the egg, orange juice and vanilla. Knead until dough forms a ball. Wrap in foil and refrigerate for 2 ½ hours.

5 FILLINGS:

1. Jam. Use seedless preserves of many flavors. Don't use jelly, as it becomes watery.

2. Poppy seed

    2/3 cup poppy seeds

    1/3 cup water

    3 tbsp. honey

    ¼ cup finely chopped walnuts

    ½ tsp. zest of lemon

    2 tbsp. sugar

    Mix 2 tbsp. honey and rest of ingredients in a small saucepan. Simmer until it thickens. Stir in rest of honey. Cool

3. Chocolate chips

4. Raisins

5. Apricot or Prune, uncooked

    16 pitted apricots or prunes

    1 tsp. grated lemon rind

    1 tbsp. lemon juice

    2 tbsp. honey

Place first 3 ingredients in a food processor and process until smooth. Add enough honey to bind mixture together.

ASSEMBLY:

Preheat oven to 350⁰. Coat 2 cookie sheets with non-stick spray.

On a lightly floured board, roll a section of dough to 1/8" thickness. Cut into 3" circles with a cookie cutter or a glass. Place a teaspoon of desired filling in the center. Fold into a triangle by pinching the edges together. Bake for 20 minutes.

OPTIONAL GLAZE:

1 egg white, 1 tbsp. sugar and ½ tsp. cinnamon

Beat egg whites in a small bowl until frothy. Brush on tops of uncooked hamentashen. Combine sugar and cinnamon and sprinkle over egg white. Bake immediately.

FAVORITE COOKIES, BARS and CANDY

SNICKERDOODLES

1 cup margarine
1 ½ cups sugar
2 eggs
2 ¾ cups sifted flour
1 tsp. cream of tartar
¼ tsp. salt
Rolling mixture: 2 tbsp. sugar, 1 tsp. each of cinnamon and cloves.

Mix margarine sugar and eggs thoroughly. Sift together flour, soda, cream of tartar and salt. Add to first mixture. Form walnut-sized balls. Roll with sugar mixture and place 2" apart in an ungreased baking sheet. Bake about 10-12 minutes at 400⁰ until edges are lightly browned. The cookies will puff up and then flatten out with crinkled tops. Let stand a few minutes and cool completely on a rack.

OLD-FASHIONED SUGAR COOKIES

(Use this recipe to make decorated Chanukah cut-outs. About 3 dozen)

½ cup sugar
½ cup powdered sugar
½ cup margarine
½ cup salad oil
½ tsp. vanilla
½ tsp. cream of tartar
1 egg
2 ¼ cups sifted flour
¼ tsp. salt
½ tsp. baking soda
More sugar for rolling

Mix first 4 ingredients. Add the egg. Sift flour, salt, cream of tartar and soda. Add to mixture. Add vanilla. Dough will be soft. Roll into walnut-sized balls. Roll balls in white sugar. Place in a greased baking sheet. Flatten cookies with the bottom of a glass dipped in sugar. Bake 10-12 minutes at 350⁰. Remove from sheet immediately to avoid crumbling.

CHOCOLATE CHIP COOKIES

1 cup sugar
1 cup brown sugar
1 cup butter or margarine, softened
2 eggs
1 ½ tsp. vanilla
3 cups flour
1 tsp. salt
1 tsp. baking soda
12 oz. semisweet chocolate chips

Beat together, by hand or machine, the first 5 ingredients up to vanilla. Sift flour, salt and baking soda together. Gradually add flour mixture to sugar mixture. Add chocolate chips and mix well. Drop by teaspoonfuls on a greased baking sheet, 2" apart. Bake at 375⁰ for 10-12 minutes.

VARIATION: Add ½ cup chopped walnuts or coconut.

PEANUT BUTTER COOKIES 1

½ cup margarine
1 cup honey (oil cup first)
1 cup peanut butter
2 cups whole wheat flour
1 tsp. baking powder
1 tsp. soda
½ tsp. salt

Cream margarine, honey, and, peanut butter. Stir in dry ingredients. Form walnut-sized balls and place on a lightly greased baking sheet. Flatten cookies with a flour-dipped fork, making a crisscross pattern. Bake 10-12 minutes at 375⁰.

PEANUT BUTTER COOKIES 2

½ cup peanut butter
½ cup margarine, softened
½ cup sugar
½ cup brown sugar
1 egg
½ tsp. vanilla
1¼ cups flour
½ tsp. baking soda
¼ tsp. salt

Cream peanut butter and butter until smooth. Add sugars, egg, and vanilla. Beat 1 minute. Sift flour, soda and salt together. Gradually add to sugar mixture. Make 1" balls. Place on a baking sheet 2" apart. Press flat with a fork in a crisscross pattern. Bake at 375⁰ for 10-12 minutes until golden brown.

OATMEAL RAISIN COOKIES

(4 dozen)
1¾ cups flour
¾ tsp. each of baking powder and soda
½ tsp. each of salt, cinnamon and nutmeg
1 cup unsalted butter, softened
¼ cup sugar
1 ½ cups brown sugar
2 large eggs
2½ tsp. vanilla
1 cup raisins, chopped
3 ½ cups rolled oats

Preheat oven to 350° and spray oil on cookie sheets.

Mix flour, baking powder, soda and seasonings. In a large bowl, blend butter, sugars, eggs and vanilla. Add the flour mixture and then the raisins and rolled oats. Form 1½ " balls and place on baking sheet 2 inches apart. Flatten balls to ½" thickness. Bake 1 sheet at a time until cookies are light brown, 12-14 minutes.

PUMPKIN COOKIES

½ cup margarine
1 ¼ cups brown sugar
2 eggs
1 ½ cups canned pumpkin, no spices
½ tsp. salt
¼ tsp. ginger
½ tsp. each of nutmeg and cinnamon
2 ½ cups cake flour
4 tsp. baking powder
1 cup raisins
1 cup chopped nuts
1 tsp. lemon extract

Cream thoroughly the margarine and sugar. Add and blend well eggs, pumpkin and seasonings. Sift flour and baking powder together. Stir in raisins and nuts. Add flour mixture to creamed mixture and beat. Stir in lemon extract. Drop by teaspoonfuls onto greased cookie sheet. Bake 15 minutes at 400°. (36 cookies)

MEXICAN WEDDING CAKES

2 cups sifted cake flour
1/8 tsp. salt
¾ cup butter or margarine
4 tbsp. powdered sugar and more for rolling
2 tsp. vanilla

1 tsp. cold water
1 cup finely chopped pecans

Sift flour with salt.

Cream the butter until fluffy. Add sugar, vanilla and cold water. Stir in flour and pecans. Wrap dough in waxed paper and chill. Shape into 1" balls and bake for 6 minutes at 400⁰ or until lightly browned. Cool slightly before rolling in powdered sugar. (3 ½-4 dozen)

MEXICAN CINNAMON BALLS

1 cup butter, softened
½ cup powdered sugar
2 ¼ cups sifted flour
1 tsp. cinnamon
1 tsp. vanilla
¼ tsp salt
For rolling cookies:
½ cup granulated or powdered sugar with ½ tsp. cinnamon

Beat butter at high speed with electric mixer until fluffy. At low speed, beat in sugar, flour, cinnamon, vanilla and salt until combined. Shape into a large ball, wrap in waxed paper and refrigerate 30 minutes.

Preheat oven to 400 degrees. Roll dough into ¾" balls. Place on ungreased cookie sheets 1 ½ inches apart. Bake 10 minutes until golden brown. Roll hot cookies in cinnamon-sugar mixture. Makes about 5 dozen

CHOCOLATE JIFFIES

1½ cups sifted flour
1 tsp. baking powder
½ tsp. salt
2 eggs
½ cup vegetable oil
1 cup sugar
2 squares chocolate, melted
1 tsp. vanilla
Walnut halves

Sift the dry ingredients together. Beat the eggs and add the oil, sugar, melted chocolate and vanilla. Blend well. Add to dry ingredients. Drop by teaspoonfuls onto a greased cookie sheet. Top each jcookie with a walnut half. Bake for 12 minutes in a 325⁰ oven.

CHOCOLATE CORNFLAKE BARS

1 cup each of semi-sweet chocolate chips and butterscotch chips
½ cup peanut butter
5 cups corn flakes, regular or gluten-free

Place all the chips in a large saucepan and stir until smooth over low heat. Remove from heat and add corn flakes. Stir until completely coated. Using waxed paper, press the mixture evenly into a 9x9x2" pan sprayed with oil. Cut into about 32 bars when cool.

MUD BARS

1¼ cups flour
½ tsp. baking soda
½ tsp. salt
¾ cup brown sugar, packed
½ cup butter, softened
1 tsp. vanilla
1 egg
2 cups semi-sweet chocolate chips, divided
½ cup chopped walnuts or pecans

Preheat oven to 375⁰. Combine flour, soda, and salt in a small bowl. In a large bowl, mix brown sugar, butter, and vanilla until creamy. Add egg and mix well. Gradually add flour mixture. Stir in 1 1/3 cups chocolate chips and nuts. Spread into a foil-lines 9x9" pan. Bake about 25 minutes. Remove from oven and top with rest of chips. When chips look shiny, spread them out with a spatula. Cool and let set before cutting into bars.

LEMON BARS

1 1/3 cups flour
¼ cup sugar
½ cup butter or margarine, softened
2 eggs
¾ cup sugar
2 tbsp. flour
¼ tsp. baking powder
3 tbsp. lemon juice

Combine first 3 ingredients in a bowl to make the crust. Beat until coarse crumbs form. Press into bottom of an 8x8' pan. Bake in preheated oven at 350⁰ for 15 minutes until lightly browned. Combine the remaining ingredients to make the filling. Beat at low speed until mixed well. Pour over hot crust. Continue baking about 20 minutes until filling is set. Cool and sprinkle with powdered sugar, if desired.

QUICK BROWNIES

2 cups sugar
1¾ cups flour
½ cup cocoa
1 tsp. salt
5 eggs
1 cup vegetable oil

1 tsp. vanilla
1 cup semisweet chocolate chips

Combine the first 7 ingredients in a large bowl. Mix well until smooth. Pour into a 13x9x2" pan. Sprinkle with chocolate chips and bake at 350⁰ for 30 minutes or until an inserted toothpick comes out clean. Cool and cut into about 36 brownies.

NO-BAKE OAT BARS

1 cup quick oats

1/3 cup dried cherries or cranberries
½ cup peanut butter or almond butter
3 tbsp. honey
1 tsp. vanilla

Mix all together and spread out in a pan. Refrigerate for 2 hours and cut into bars.

CHOCOLATE CHERRY MASH

1 cup sugar
2 tbsp. butter or margarine
¼ tsp. salt
1/3 cup undiluted evaporated milk
1 cup miniature marshmallows
1 cup cherry chips (hard to find—go on-line)
1 cup chocolate chips
1.2 cup peanut butter
1 cup salted Spanish peanuts

Combine sugar, butter, salt and milk in a 2 quart saucepan. Boil over medium heat for 5 minutes, stirring occasionally. Stir in marshmallows and cherry chips. Spread in an 8"or 9" square pan, lined with wax paper. Melt chocolate chips with peanut butter in a small pan over low heat, stirring together. Stir in peanuts. Spread over cherry layer. When cool, cut into squares.

YUMMY FUDGE

2 cups sugar
¼ cup honey
½ tsp. salt
1 1/3 cups undiluted evaporated milk
1 (12 0z.) pkg. semi sweet chocolate chips
1 cup miniature marshmallows
1 cup nuts (optional)
1 tsp. vanilla

In a heavy saucepan combine honey, sugar, salt and milk. Bring to a rolling boil over medium heat, stirring constantly. Reduce heat and continue boiling 8 minutes. Remove from heat. Add marshmallows and chocolate. Beat until smooth and mixture starts to thicken. Mix in nuts, if desired, and vanilla. Pour into a buttered 9" square pan. Cool in refrigerator before cutting into squares.

MICROWAVE FUDGE

¾ cup margarine
3 cups sugar
2/3 cup evaporated milk
1 pkg. (12 oz.) semi-sweet chocolate chips
1 jar (7 oz.) marshmallow crème
1 cup chopped nuts
1 tsp. vanilla

Microwave margarine in a 4-quart microwave-safe bowl on HIGH 1 minute or until melted. Add sugar and milk; mix well. Microwave this on HIGH 5 minutes or until boiling begins, stirring after 3 minutes. Stir in chips until melted. Add remaining ingredients and mix well. Pour into a greased 9" squae pan. Cool at room temperature. Cut into squares. Refrigerate.

PEANUT BUTTER FUDGE

2 cups sugar
½ cup milk
1 1/3 cup peanut butter, creamy or chunky to taste
1 jar (7 oz.) marshmallow crème

Bring sugar and milk to a boil in a saucepan. Boil 3 minutes and add peanut butter and marshmallow crème. Mix well. Pour quickly into a buttered 8" square pan. Chill before cutting into squares.

POPCORN BALLS

2 cups granulated sugar
1½ cups water
½ tsp. salt
½ cup light corn syrup
1 tsp. vinegar
1 tsp. vanilla
5 quarts popped corn

Butter sides of a saucepan. In it combine sugar, water, salt, syrup and vinegar. Cook to hard ball stage (250°). Stir in vanilla. Slowly pour over popped corn, stirring just to mix well. Butter hands lightly and shape balls. Makes 15-20 balls

PEANUT BRITTLE

2 cups sugar
1 cup light corn syrup
¼ tsp. salt
½ cup water
2 cups unsalted peanuts
1 tsp. margarine
1 tsp. vanilla
2 tsp. baking soda

Grease a large jelly roll pan (15x10"). In a large saucepan, bring sugar, syrup, salt and ½ cup water to boil, stirring constantly until sugar dissolves. Continue cooking without stirring until candy thermometer reads 300⁰. Remove from heat; stir in peanuts, margarine, and vanilla. Sprinkle baking soda over this and stir in quickly. Pour into pan, spreading evenly with a rubber spatula. Let stand 30 minutes until cooled and hardened. Remove brittle from pan and break into pieces. Store brittle in a tightly covered container for up to 2 weeks. Makes 2 pounds

CAKES, PIES and OTHER DESSERTS

APPLE CAKE

4-5 large apples, peeled, cored and sliced thin
2 tsp. cinnamon
2 cups sugar
4 large eggs
1 cup oil
½ cup orange juice
1 ½ tsp. vanilla
3 cups flour
1 tbsp. baking powder
½ tsp. salt

Place apples in a large bowl. Sprinkle with cinnamon and ½ cup of the sugar. Beat the eggs in another bowl. Add the rest of the sugar, the oil, orange juice and vanilla. Sift together the flour, baking powder and salt. Combine both mixtures.

Grease a 10" tube pan and dust with flour. Pour in 1/3 of the batter and layer 1/3 of the apples on top. Repeat this twice with a layer of apples on top. Bake at 350⁰ for 1½ hours until golden. Let cool before removing from pan.

APPLESAUCE CAKE

2 cups sugar
1 cup margarine
2 ½ cups thick applesauce
3 cups flour
3 tsp. baking soda
2 tbsp. cocoa
1 tsp. cinnamon
1 cup raisins

Cream the sugar and margarine together. Add applesauce. Sift dry ingredients together and add to applesauce mixture. Stir in the raisins. Grease a 9x13" pan. Pour batter and bake about 1 hour at 350⁰.

Cool cake. Server plain or dust with powdered sugar.

CARROT CAKE

2 cups flour
2 cups sugar
2 tsp. each: baking powder and baking soda
1 tsp. salt
2 tsp. cinnamon

1 1/4 cup oil
4 eggs
3 cups grated carrots
2 tsp. vanilla
1 ½ cups walnut

Sift together the first 6 ingredients and place in a bowl. Add the oil and eggs, one at a time. Mix well after each egg. Batter will be very thick. Stir in the carrots, vanilla and nuts. Pour into a greased and floured 9x13" pan. Bake at 350⁰ for 50-60 minutes. Let cool before frosting. Refrigerate it afterwards.

Cream Cheese Frosting:

4 oz. cream cheese, softened
1 ½ cups powdered sugar
1 tsp. vanilla
4 tbsp. butter or margarine

Mix the above ingredients until smooth.

ANGEL FOOD CAKE

1 cup (8-10) egg whites
¼ tsp. cream of tartar
1 ¼ cups sifted sugar
¾ tsp. vanilla
¼ tsp. salt
¼ tsp. almond extract
1 cup cake flour, sifted 2-4 times

Beat egg whites with salt in an electric mixer, preferably with a wire whisk attachment. When foamy, add the cream of tartar. Continue beating until eggs are stiff and form peaks. Fold in sugar, adding 2 tablespoons at a time. Fold in flavorings. Sift a small amount of flour over the mixture. Fold in and continue until all flour is used. Pour batter into an ungreased tube pan. Bake at 325⁰ for 50 minutes until done. Remove from oven and invert to cool.

RUM CAKE

1 cup chopped pecans
1 18oz. pkg. yellow cake mix
1 3 3/4oz. pkg. instant vanilla pudding
4 eggs
½ cup cold water
½ cup vegetable oil
½ cup dark rum

Preheat oven to 325 degrees. Grease and flour a 10" tube pan or 12 cup Bundt pan. Sprinkle the nuts over the bottom. Mix the cake ingredients. Pour over the nuts. Bake 1 hour. Cool. Invert on a serving plate. Prick the top with a toothpick or fork. Drizzle and smooth the glaze evenly over the top and sides. Allow cake to absorb the glaze and repeat until the glaze is used up.

GLAZE:

¼ lb. butter
¼ cup water
1 cup granulated sugar
½ cup dark rum

Melt butter in a saucepan. Stir in water and sugar. Boil 5 minutes, stirring. Remove from heat and stir in rum.

BASIC DEVIL'S FOOD CAKE

1/2 cup margarine or butter
1 ¼ cups brown sugar
2 eggs, unbeaten or egg substitute equivalent
3 oz. bitter chocolate, melted
2 cups cake flour
2 tsp. baking soda
1 tsp. vanilla
1 cups milk

Cream the butter. Add sugar gradually until mixture is fluffy. Add eggs, one at a time, blending well after each egg. Add melted chocolate and blend. Sift flour and add soda. Sift again. Add to batter, alternately with the milk. Add vanilla. Pour into 2 8-inch layer pans. Bake at 350⁰ until done, about 25-30 minutes.

GLAZE:

1 cup powdered sugar
2 tbsp. baking cocoa
2 tbsp. orange juice
½ tsp. vanilla extract

BANANA CAKE

4 oz. sweet chocolate
2 ½ cups flour
½ tsp. salt
½ tsp. baking powder
6 oz. butter
1 ½ cups sugar
1 cup buttermilk or sour cream
3 eggs
2 bananas, mashed
1 tsp. vanilla

Melt chocolate. Cream the butter and sugar together. Add eggs and bananas. Mix in the flour and buttermilk, alternately. Add chocolate and vanilla. Bake in a 13x9" pan or 2x8" cake pans at 350⁰ for 30-40 minutes. Frost and garnish with sliced bananas.

NOTE: Make your own buttermilk by whisking together 3 parts plain yogurt and 1part milk for the desired amount of buttermilk.

PINEAPPLE UPSIDE-DOWN CAKE

1 can pineapple rings in juice
2/3 cups brown sugar
¼ cup melted butter or margarine
8-10 maraschino cherries
1 pkg. yellow cake mix, prepared according to pkg. directions

Drain pineapple and reserve ¾ cup juice. Combine melted butter and brown sugar in a 13x9' baking pan. Arrange pineapple rings over sugar mixture. Put a cherry in each ring. Prepare the cake mix, replacing some of the water with the reserved pineapple juice. Pour batter over pineapple and bake in a 350⁰ oven 35-40 minutes, or until done. Cool, loosen edges and invert onto a serving platter.

ORANGE CAKE

1¼ cups flour
1 ½ tsp. baking powder
½ cup sugar
6 tbsp. butter or margarine
2 eggs
1 tbsp. orange juice
Grated rind of 1 orange

Grease and flour a square cake pan. Sift flour and baking powder together. Place all ingredients in a large bowl and stir gently until softened and then, cream briskly for 2 minutes. Pour mixture into prepared pan. Level the top. Bake at 350 degrees for 55-60 minutes. Cake is done when no impression is left after pressing top gently with a finger. Take out and cool. Cut in slices. Eat soon or refrigerate.

CHERRY CHEESECAKE

CRUST:

1 9" graham cracker crumb crust, purchased

Or make your own crust:

6 tbsp. butter or margarine, preferably unsalted

1 1/4 cups finely crushed graham crackers (or vanilla or chocolate wafers), from pkg. or grind in processor

1/4-1/2 cup sugar, depending on sweetness of crackers or cookies

Melt butter in a 9" pie plate and cool slightly. Add crushed graham crackers and sugar. Stir until moistened. Press mixture firmly against bottom and sides of pie plate. Try pressing another pie pan on top to make thickness even. Scoop up any excess and put it back or use for topping. Bake for 10 minutes at 350⁰. Cool before filling.

FILLING:

1 8-oz. pkg. cream cheese, softened
1 small pkg. instant vanilla pudding mix
2 cups cold milk

Stir cream cheese until very soft. Blend in 1/2 cup milk. Add the rest of milk and pudding mix. Beat 1 minute slowly with an egg beater just until well blended. Pour into crust and chill 1 hour or until set.

TOPPING:

1 can (21 oz.) cherry pie filling, chilled. Top the pie with cherries prior to serving.

SOY CHEESECAKE

1 8 oz. pkg. soy cream cheese (Try Tofutti Better Than Cream Cheese)
1/2 cup sugar
1/2 tsp. vanilla
4 egg whites
1 9" graham cracker crust
Fruit jelly for topping, optional

Beat soy cream cheese, vanilla and sugar until blended. Use medium speed if using an electric mixer. Add the egg whites and mix just until blended. Pour into crust. Bake at 350⁰ for 40 minutes or until set in the middle. Cool and refrigerate for at least 3 hours. When ready to serve, heat the jelly and drizzle over cheesecake, if desired.

PUMPKIN PIE

1 cup sugar
1 1/2 tsp. cinnamon
1/2 tsp. cloves
1/2 tsp. allspice

½ tsp. nutmeg

½ tsp. ginger

1//2 tsp. salt

2 eggs

1 ½ cups pumpkin

1 2/3 cups evaporated milk

1 9" unbaked pie shell

Blend sugar and spices and salt together. Beat eggs with pumpkin and evaporated milk. Combine sugar mixture with pumpkin mixture and b lend well. Pour into pie shell and bake at 425⁰ for 15 minutes. Reduce heat to 350⁰ and continue baking 35-40 minutes. Cool.

NO-BAKE LAYERED PUMPKIN PIE

1 graham cracker crust

4 oz. cream cheese, softened

1 tbsp. milk

1 tbsp. sugar

1 8 oz. tub frozen non-dairy whipped topping, thawed

1 cup cold milk

2 small pkgs. vanilla instant pudding

1 can of pumpkin (16 oz.)

1 tsp. cinnamon

½ tsp. ginger

¼ tsp. cloves

In a large bowl, whisk cream cheese, 1 tablespoon milk and sugar until smooth. Stir in ½ of the whipped topping and spread this on the bottom of the crust. Pour 1 cup milk into a bowl. Add the pudding mixes and beat 1 minute with a wire whisk until thick. Stir in pumpkin and spices. Spread over cream cheese layer. Refrigerate for 3-4 hours or until set. Top with remaining whipped topping.

ALMOND MILK PUMPKIN PIE

Filling:

¾ cup sugar

1 ¼ tsp. cinnamon

½ tsp. salt

¼ tsp. ginger

1/8 tsp. each: ground nutmeg and cloves

1 can (15oz.) of pumpkin

2 large eggs

1¼ cup almond milk

Mix sugar, salt and spices in a large bowl. Add pumpkin, almond milk, and eggs. Blend well. Pour into unbaked pastry shell. Set pie on bottom rack of a 425⁰ oven. Bake for 15 minutes. Reduce temperature to 350⁰ and continue baking about 45 minutes until center of pie is set. Cool on a wire rack at least 2 hours. Chill after serving in an airtight container.

Pastry Crust:

1 single-crust 9" pastry shell, purchased (thawed if frozen) or make your own:

> 1 cup sifted flour
>
> ½ tsp. salt
>
> 1/3 cup shortening
>
> 2 tbsp. water

Sift flour and salt together. Work ½ of the shortening into flour with a fork or pastry blender. When mixture looks like coarse meal, add the rest of the shortening and cut until mixture looks like large peas.

Gradually stir in water, 1 tablespoon at a time. Roll on a lightly floured board to 1/8" thickness.. Fit loosely into 9" pan. Fold extra pastry under and pinch with finger to flute the edge.

Gingersnap Crust:

> 22 gingersnaps, crumbled
>
> 2 tbsp. sugar
>
> ¼ cup melted butter

Ina small bowl, mix crumbs and sugar. Stir in butter. Press mixture firmly and evenly against bottom and sides of pie plate. Bake 5 minutes at 350⁰. Cool on wire rack.

FAVORITE APPLE PIE

Pastry for 9" double-crust pie, deep dish
10 large apples (8 cups) Golden, Red Delicious, Granny Smith or Galas (use a combination)
1 ½ cups sugar
3-4 tbsp. flour, depending on juiciness of apples
2 tsp. cinnamon
½ tsp. nutmeg
Dash of salt
1 tbsp. butter
A little milk and sugar for top crust

Peel, core and thinly slice apples.

Mix sugar, flour, spices and salt separately. Sift dry mixture over apples and mix thoroughly. Line a pie plate with crust and place apples in stacks carefully. Cut butter into small pieces to arrange evenly over apples. Place top crust over apples, pinch edges, and then coat with a light covering of milk. Sprinkle top crust with sugar ant cut a design in top crust. Bake in a 400⁰ oven for 1 hour, or until done.

TIP: If edges start getting too brown, place foil or a metal pie ring around it.

LEMON MERINGUE PIE

1 9" graham cracker crust
3 eggs, separated
1 can (14 oz.) sweetened condensed milk
½ cup lemon juice
1 tsp. grated lemon rind
¼ tsp. cream of tartar
1/3 cup sugar

Preheat oven to 350⁰. In a medium bowl, beat egg yolks. Stir in the milk, lemon juice and rind. Pour into crust.

Meringue:

In a small bowl, beat egg whites with cream of tartar until foamy. Gradually add sugar, beating until whites are stiff but not dry. Spread meringue on top of pie, sealing carefully to edge of crust.

Bake 12-15 minutes or until meringue turns golden brown. Cool and chill before serving. Refrigerate afterwards.

EASY CHERRY PIE

2 9" pie shells
4 cups sour cherries, fresh or canned
3 tbsp. tapioca
1 tsp. cinnamon
1-1 1/3 cup sugar to taste
2 tbsp. butter

Combine cherries and tapioca. Add sugar and let stand 10-15 minutes. Pour cherry mixture into pie shell and dot with butter. Roll out second crust and cut into strips to form a lattice top over filling. Sprinkle with sugar. Bake at 450⁰ for 10 minutes. Bake another 40-45 minutes in a 350⁰ oven. Cool on a wire rack.

FLAN (CARAMEL CUSTARD)

1/3 cup sugar
6 eggs
6 tbsp. sugar
2 cups milk
1 tsp. vanilla
Hot water

Heat 1/3 cup sugar in a small frying pan over moderate heat until it melts. Shake the pan instead of stirring. As soon as sugar is a dark caramelized color, pour at once into bottom of a 9" cake pan or pie pan. Set aside.

Preheat oven to 350⁰. Beat eggs and 6 tbsp. sugar together. Add milk and vanilla. Pour ½" of very hot water into a pan larger than cake pan. Place cake pan in hot water bath and pour in the egg mixture.

Bake for 25-35 minutes. The custard is done when a knife inserted halfway between edge and center comes out clean.

Remove from hot water and chill at once. When cold and ready to serve, run a knife around the custard edge to loosen it. Cover with a rimmed serving plate. Holding plate, firmly, invert the flan. It will slip out and the caramel sauce will flow. Cut into wedges and spoon on the sauce. Refrigerate leftovers.

BREAD PUDDING

1½ cups milk
¼ cup sugar
1 tsp. vanilla
¼ tsp. salt
2 eggs
4 cups white bread cubes
½ cup seedless raisins
1 tbsp. butter or margarine cut in small pieces
1 tsp. cinnamon

Grease a 9" square baking dish. In a large bowl, beat m ilk, sugar, vanilla, salt and eggs with a wire whisk until well blended. Add bread, raisins and butter and toss to coat. Let stand 5-10 minutes, then pour into baking dish and sprinkle with cinnamon. Bake in a preheated 350°oven 50-60 minutes until a knife inserted in center comes out clean. Serve with ice cream or whipped topping.

FRUIT and FRUIT DESSERTS

BANANAS FOSTER

2 peeled ripe bananas cut in half lengthwise
1 tbsp. butter or margarine
2 tbsp. dark brown sugar
2 tbsp. dark rum
Garnish: sour cream or ice cream and chopped nuts, optional

Melt the butter in a large nonstick skillet over medium heat. Add the sugar and stir until it dissolves.

Add the bananas and cook 2 minutes on each side until golden. Remove to plates. Add the rum to the skillet and simmer 30 seconds. Pour sauce over bananas. Garnish as desired.

BERRY CRISP 1

4 cups whole blueberries or sliced strawberries
1 cup sifted flour
¾ cup sugar
½ tsp. cinnamon
½ cup mayonnaise

Grease an 8x8x2" baking pan. Place fruit in pan. Stir flour, sugar and cinnamon together. Add mayonnaise until mixture looks like coarse crumbles. Sprinkle over fruit. Bake crisp in a 400⁰ oven 40 minutes or until browned.

BERRY CRISP 2

4 cups berries
1 ½ cups graham cracker crumbs
2 tbsp. honey
2 tbsp. brown sugar
¼ tsp. cinnamon
1/8 tsp. nutmeg
¼ cup butter or margarine

Melt butter in a saucepan. Stir in crumbs and slowly add the brown sugar, honey and spices. Mix well. Pour berries into a greased oven dish or pan. Add more sugar if desired. Top with the graham cracker mixture. Bake in a preheated 350⁰ oven for 20 minutes. Serve with ice cream.

PEACH CRUMBLE

2 cans (15 oz.) peaches
½ tsp. cinnamon
½ cup flour
1/3 cup brown sugar, packed
1/3 cup old-fashioned oats
1/3 cup walnuts
1/3 cup butter or margarine, softened

Place fruit in an 8x8" baking dish. Combine flour, cinnamon, sugar, oats and nuts. Mix in butter until crumbly and sprinkle over fruit. Bake at 425⁰ for 15 minutes or until golden. Serve with ice cream or whipped topping.

WATERMELON BOWL

1 large watermelon, fully ripe
Filling:
Watermelon, honeydew and cantaloupe balls
2-3 cups fresh strawberries, washed, hulled and halved
2 cups seedless grapes, halved
Pitted fresh cherries or other fruit in season such as blueberries, peaches, pineapple wedges or kiwi
Dressing, optional:
¼ cup sugar
¼ cup fresh lemon juice
¼ cup lime juice
1 tsp. grated lime peel

Cut watermelon 1" above the middle, lengthwise. Cut a design edge with scallops or triangles, if desired. Cut out the fruit with a melon ball cutter. Remove seeds and remaining pink meat. Drain well. Fill with fruit. Keep bowl chilled until ready to serve.

WATERMELON BOWL

BAKED APPLES

4 medium Granny Smith or other baking apples
Cinnamon
18 miniature marshmallows
4 tbsp. brown sugar

Core apples, but don't cut all the way through. Peel apples if so desired. Wrap apples with heavy foil after sprinkling centers with cinnamon and filling alternately with marshmallows and brown sugar. Seal foil together. Bake in a 350⁰ oven for 30-35 minutes until tender. Unwrap carefully.

FRESH FRUIT DRESSINGS

1. Mint Dressing: For 7-8 cups of fruit, combine 2 containers of plain yogurt, ½ cup sifted powdered sugar, and 2 drops mint extract. Chill. Garnish fruit with mint sprigs.

2. Fruit Dip: Mix 8 oz. fat free cream cheese, 1 container flavored low-fat yogurt and lemon zest to taste.

DESSERT FRUIT SAUCE

(Use to top pound cake, angel food cake, crepes or ice cream)

Combine ¾ cup pineapple juice, 1 tbsp. cornstarch and 1 tbsp. sugar in a saucepan and heat to boiling. Stir in 1 ½ cups fresh or frozen raspberries. Continue cooking until heated thoroughly and sauce thickens.

ROSH HASHONA STEWED APPLES

3-4 large apples
Juice of ½ a lemon
¼ cup sugar
¼ tsp. cinnamon
½ cup water

Wash, peel and core apples. Slice the apples and place in a flat pan. Add sugar, water, lemon juice and cinnamon. Toss the apple slices gently. Cook until tender over medium heat about 3-5 minutes, depending on how thick the slices are. To glaze, cook until the syrup thickens. Serve warm or chilled.

MY FAVORITE PASSOVER RECIPES

MEGINA/MATZA MEAT PIE

Meat mixture:
2 lbs. ground beef
1 small onion, chopped fine
1 tsp. salt
½ tsp. pepper
2 tbsp. oil
½ cup chopped parsley
5 beaten eggs

Heat the oil and brown the meat and onions with salt and pepper. After cooling, add the beaten eggs and parsley. Set aside.

Matzos Lining: (for 9x13pan)

8 sheets matzos
4-5 eggs
Spray oil
Water for soaking

Beat 3 of the eggs and pour onto a small baking sheet. Soak 4 matzos in warm water until they are soft but not falling apart. Drain excess water. Gently pick up 1 matzo and dip both sides in the egg. Begin lining the pan. Don't worry if the matzo breaks. Just patch with more matzo. Repeat until bottom and sides of pan are lined.

Fill the pan with the meat mixture. Spread evenly. Beat more eggs. Soak more matzos. (You probably only need 3 but allow for breakage. Make fried matzos with any leftovers.) Top the meat with a layer of the matzo. Bake for 30-40 minutes at 400⁰. (Optional: When done, pour ½ cup of chicken broth over the top.)

MEGINA

QUASHJADU DE CARNE/ MEAT CASSEROLE

2 lbs. ground beef
1 chopped onion
2 tbsp. oil
2 tsp. salt or to taste
1 tsp. pepper or to taste
2 broken up matzo, soaked in warm water and squeezed dry
10 eggs

Grease a 9x13" pan. Brown the meat and onion in the oil. When cool, add the seasoning, parsley and farfel. Beat 8 eggs and blend well with the meat. Pour the mixture into the pan.

Beat 2 more eggs and spread over the top. Bake for 30 minutes at 400⁰.

VARIATION: Mix last 2 eggs with a cup of mashed potato.

ROAST LEG OF LAMB

1 5-6 lb. leg of lamb
2 cloves garlic
2 tbsp. olive oil
1 tbsp. chopped rosemary
¾ tsp. salt
¾ tsp. pepper
Grated zest of 1 lemon
1 cup water

Preheat oven to 350⁰. Trim fat from leg. Slice garlic cloves thinly lengthwise. With a knife make several gashes all over the leg and insert the garlic slices. Place the leg in a large roasting pan, meatier side up. Combine oil, salt, pepper and rosemary and lemon zest. Rub all over leg. Add 1 cup water to pan and roast 1 ½-2 hrs until internal temperature is150⁰ for medium or 160⁰ for medium well. Transfer lamb to a warm plate. Cover loosely with foil and let stand 15 minutes before carving. Serve with gravy from drippings or with mint jelly (my family's favorite).

VARIATION: Roast lamb in a rotisserie.

QUASHJADU DE ESPINACA/ SPINACH BAKE

2 ½ lbs. cleaned spinach
8 large eggs
Farfel (2 squares matzos soaked in warm water which is squeezed out)
2 cups grated parmesan (reserve ¼ cup for the topping)
1 cup crumbled feta
1 tsp. salt (optional)

Preheat oven to 400⁰.

Wash and chop the spinach. Mix with the remaining ingredients in a large bowl. Grease a 9x13 pan. Fill it with the spinach mixture. Top with reserved cheese and bake for 40-50 minutes until browned lightly.

KIFTES DE PRASA/ LEEK PATTIES

5-6 stalks leeks
1 cup mashed potatoes
3 tbsp. matzo meal
2 eggs
1 onion, chopped (optional)
1 tsp. salt and pepper to taste
Vegetable oil for frying

Cut off tops and trim bottoms of stalks. Wash well, especially hidden dirt between leaves. Cut stalks in half lengthwise and chop in one inch cuts across. Throw into a large pot filled with cold water. Stir to loosen dirt. Drain. Repeat if leeks are very dirty. Cook leeks and onion in a large pot with water until very tender about 30-40 minutes. Drain well. Squeeze excess water out. Chop or mash the leeks. I use a potato masher. You can use a food processor, also. Mix in the other ingredients. If not very thick, add more matzo meal. Form patties 1 ½ inch in diameter and fry both sides in hot oil 5-6 at a time, keeping temperature high. Drain on paper towels. Serve hot or cold. Some squeeze lemon on before serving.

VARIATIONS:

1. Leek patties are traditionally served also on Rosh Hashona. Use bread crumbs instead of matzo meal.
2. Add ½ lb. ground meat before frying. Serve with heated sauce of 1 8oz. can tomato sauce, 2 tbsp. oil, juice of½ lemon, salt and ground pepper to taste.

KIFTES DE SALMON/ SALMON PATTIES

2 cans (6-7 oz.) pink salmon, drained and flaked
¼ cup matzo meal
1/4 cup chopped parsley
2 beaten eggs
2 tbsp. grated onion
Salt and pepper to taste
Oil for frying

Mix everything except oil together. Shape into flattened patties, about ten. Fry both sides in hot oil until golden brown. Drain on paper towels. Eat alone or heated with the tomato sauce above.

FRITADA S DE PATATA/POTATO FRITTERS

3 large potatoes
3 beaten eggs
¼ cup matzo meal
1 cup grated parmesan or kasseri cheese
1 tsp. salt and pepper to taste
Oil for frying

Peel, boil and mash the potatoes. Beat the eggs and add to potatoes with cheese, salt and pepper. Form patties and fry both sides in oil. Drain excess oil by placing patties on paper towels.

FRIED MATZOS

3 matzos
1 egg, beaten
½ tsp. salt
Oil for frying

Break and soak the matzos in warm water until soft. Drain and squeeze out moisture. Mix with egg and salt. Grab a handful of the mixture or scoop up 1/3 cupful and slip into hot oil. Use a spatula to flatten into a pancake. Fry on both sides until golden brown. Recipe serves 2-3. Eat with syrup, honey or my family favorite: strawberry jam topped with grated kasseri cheese. A breakfast favorite with huevos haminados! (See favorite breakfasts.)

HAROSET

1 large apple, peeled, cored and sliced
1 cup pitted dates
1 cup coarsely ground walnuts
¼ cup red wine

Place apple and dates in a saucepan. Slightly cover with water and cook until most of the water has evaporated. Mash the apple and dates together to keep haroset chunky or put through a food processor for a smoother texture. For the chunky texture I like to put the nuts in a plastic baggie and pound them with a hammer to the consistency I like. Add the nuts and wine. Mix well. Play with the ingredients to get desired texture. Recipe makes 2 cups. Refrigerate until ready to serve.

MASA DE VINO/ WINE COOKIES

1 cup oil
¾ cup sweet wine
½- 3/4 cup sugar
2 cups Pesach cake meal
3 tbsp. potato starch

Blend sugar, wine and oil. Add cake meal and potato starch. Add more cake meal if too soft to handle. Make walnut-sized balls and flatten to oval shape. Make a design with fork tines. Place on baking sheet and bake at 350⁰ for about ½ hour. Recipe makes 2 1/2 -3 dozen cookies.

VARIATIONS:

1. Add a cup of chopped walnuts.

2. Roll out dough to ½ inch and cut out shapes with cookie cutters.

3. Decorate cookies with embedded walnuts.

4. Press dough into greased Madeleine moulds.

ASHUPLADOS/ MERINGUES

3 egg whites
1 cup sugar
¼ tsp. cream of tartar
¼ tsp. vanilla

Heat oven to 275⁰ and line two heavy baking sheets with parchment paper.

Separate yolks and whites of 3 eggs by cracking the eggs and letting whites slip into beater bowl. Use back and forth motion, being careful not to let yolks fall in. Reserve the yolks for another use. (Tips: Make sure bowl is dry and grease-free. Use a metal or glass bowl. Do not use a plastic bowl. Eggs at room temperature whip to a higher volume.) Beat egg whites in an electric mixer until foamy and add the cream of tartar. Keep beating, adding sugar gradually, until whites are stiff but not dry. Add the vanilla after half of the sugar has been mixed. Drop whites onto sheet by teaspoonfuls and swirl with the spoon to make a little peak. Bake meringues for about 30 minutes or until lightly browned. Cool completely and store in a tightly covered container. Recipe makes about 3 dozen.

PASSOVER BROWNIES

1 cup sugar
½ cup margarine
2 eggs
¼ cup milk
½ cup Pesach cake meal
4 tbsp. cocoa
A pinch of salt
½ cup chopped walnuts, optional

Grease a 9x9 pan. Cream the margarine and sugar. Add eggs and milk. Add the dry ingredients and mix well. Bake for 20 minutes at 300⁰ and then 10 minutes more at 325⁰. Cool and cut into squares. Recipe can de doubled.

MOUSTACHUDOS/ NUT CONFECTION

3 cups ground walnuts and almonds
1 cup sugar
1 egg, beaten
2 tbsp. orange marmalade or juice and rind of ½ orange
½ tsp cinnamon and cloves

Mix ingredients into a soft mixture easy to handle. Add a few drops of water if too thick. Moisten hands and shape into 1 inch balls. Place on a parchment lined baking sheet. Bake at 400⁰ for 10-12 minutes until lightly browned. Cool before removing with a spatula. I like to put the confection in a colorful paper cup. Recipe makes about 3 dozen.

VARIATION: Make clover shapes by pinching in twice with thumb and forefinger to make indentations.

PASSOVER NUT COOKIES

1 cup margarine
4 eggs
1 cup sugar
1 cup cake meal
½ cup chopped nuts
½ tsp. salt
2 tsp. grated lemon rind

Cream the margarine until soft. Beat in eggs and sugar until light and fluffy. Stir in cake meal, nuts, salt and lemon rind. Drop by teaspoonfuls onto well greased cookie sheets at least 2" apart. Bake in a 375⁰ oven for 10 minutes until browned at the edges. (Recipe for 4 dozen)

ALMOND MACAROONS

3 egg whites
¼ cup sugar
2 cups ground, blanched almonds
1 tbsp. matzo meal

Preheat oven to 350⁰. Cover 2 baking sheets with parchment paper. Beat egg whites until stiff. Mix the other ingredients and fold into the whites. Make balls and bake for 15-20 minutes until light brown. Makes about 2 dozen

CHOCOLATE-DIPPED COCONUT MACAROONS

1 14 oz pkg. flaked coconut
2/3 cup sugar
¼ tsp. salt
6 tbsp. cake meal
4 egg whites
1 tsp. almond extract
1 pkg. (8 squares) semi-sweet baking chocolate, melted

Mix first 4 ingredients in a large bowl. Stir in egg whites and almond extract. Blend well. Drop by tablespoonfuls onto greased cookie sheets floured (with cake meal). Bake at 325⁰ for 20 minutes until edges are golden brown. Quickly place on wire racks to cool. Dip cookies halfway into the melted chocolate. Let stand at room temperature or refrigerate on tray lined with wax paper for 30 minutes or until chocolate is firm. Makes 2 dozen

PASSOVER COOKIES

TESLIPISHTI (TURKISH PASSOVER CAKE WITH SYRUP)

9 eggs
1 cup oil
Juice of an orange
Grated rind of an orange
2 cups sugar
1 ¼ cup ground almonds or walnuts
1 lb. matzo meal

Syrup:

3 cups sugar
1½ cups water
Juice of a lemon

Beat first 5 ingredients together. Add nuts and matzo meal. Beat well. Bake in a large pan such as 11x13" at 375°
for 1 hour 15 minutes.

Combine syrup ingredients and bring to a boil. Boil to soft ball stage. Pour over hot cake.

ORANGE-NUT SPONGE CAKE

9 eggs, separated
1 ½ cups sugar
Juice and grated rind of 1 lemon
Juice and grated rind of 1 small orange
½ cup chopped walnuts
¾ cup cake meal
¾ cup potato starch
Get out a 10" tube pan. Do not grease.

In an electric mixer, beat egg whites until firm. Gradually add sugar a few tablespoons at a time and continue
beating until the whites form peaks. Set aside. Grate rinds of lemon and orange before squeezing out the juice.
Beat yolks with juices and fold into whites with a whisk or large spatula. Fold in the potato starch and cake meal.
Next, fold in the nuts and rinds. Pour into the ungreased tube pan and bake for one hour at 325°. Invert the pan
immediately and let cool. When ready to serve, use a sharp knife to loosen the sides and center of the cake from
the pan. Turn out to a serving plate or cake holder.

If cake will not be eaten in a few days, refrigerate it, as there are no preservatives and it may mold.

PASSOVER LEMON SPONGE CAKE

9 eggs, separated
2 cups sugar
6 tbsp. water
2 ½ tsp. grated lemon rind
¼ cup lemon juice

¾ cup potato starch
¾ cup cake meal
½ tsp. salt

Beat 6 yolks until frothy. Gradually add sugar until mixture is light and fluffy. Add water, lemon juice and rind. Beat thoroughly. Gradually mix in the cake meal and potato starch, blending well. Beat 6 egg whites with salt until stiff but not dry and fold gently into yolk mixture. Pour all into an ungreased tube pan. Bake in slow oven 325⁰ for 1 hour and 15 minutes or until cake springs back when lightly touched with a finger. Follow removal and serving instructions of recipe above.

TOPPING SUGGESTIONS:

1. Make strawberry sponge cake by topping with defrosted frozen strawberries and whipped cream or ice cream

2. Raspberry topping: Heat 1/3 cup raspberry preserves on low heat. Toss in 1 cup fresh or frozen raspberries (unsweetened) and mix.

PASSOVER CHEESECAKE

2 cups coconut macaroon crumbs
3 tbsp. margarine, melted
32 oz. cream cheese, softened
1 cup and 1 tsp. sugar, divided
2 tbsp. grated orange peel
4 eggs

Preheat oven to 325⁰. Lightly grease a 9-inch silver spring -form pan.

Mix cookie crumbs with margarine. Firmly press down on bottom of pan and 1 inch up the side. Bake 12 minutes. Beat cream cheese and 1 cup sugar with an electric mixer on medium speed until blended. Add peel and mix. Add eggs, 1 at a time. Mix on low speed after each egg just until blended. Pour into the crust. Bake 55 minutes or until the center is almost set. Run a knife around to loosen cake and cool before removing rim of pan. Refrigerate about 4 hours or overnight. Serve with one of the topping suggestions above.

GLUTEN-FREE CHOCOLATE CAKE

2/3 cup olive oil
6 tbsp. unsweetened cocoa
½ cup boiling water
2 tsp. vanilla extract
1 ½ cups almond meal
½ tsp. baking soda
3 large eggs
1 cup fine sugar
Pinch of salt

Preheat oven to 325⁰. Grease a 9-inch spring-form pan and line bottom with parchment paper. Mix cocoa with boiling water until smooth. Add vanilla. Set aside. Combine almond meal, soda and salt in a small bowl. Place sugar, oil and eggs in a bowl; beat in electric mixer until thickened and creamy about 3 minutes. Lower the mixer speed. Add cocoa mixture and almond meal. Scrape sides and stir before pouring into the pan. Bake until set 40-45 minutes. A cake tester or toothpick should come out fairly clean. Cool cake on a wire rack 10 minutes. Run a knife around sides to loosen. Spring cake out of pan and cool completely.

NUT BARS

3 eggs
¾ cup oil
¾ cup cake meal
¼ cup matzo meal
2 tsp. potato starch
1 cup ground nuts
1 cup sugar
Cinnamon and sugar for sprinkling

Combine ingredients. Make 3 rolls. Place on greased sheet pan. Bake 20 minutes or more at 350⁰. Slice into bars and sprinkle with cinnamon and sugar mixture. Toast for 45 minutes at 225⁰.

AMERICAN THANKSGIVING RECIPES

STUFFED TURKEY in a COVERED ROASTING PAN

(I learned how to cook my first turkey with stuffing from my then mother-in-law, Victoria (Eastern/Hasson) Carlbom.

1 whole turkey, 10-18 lbs, fresh or frozen, thawed in refrigerator
Juice of 1 lemon
Salt and pepper
Sage
1/2 cup water

BREAD STUFFING

8 cups dried bread cubes, pre-seasoned in a package
(Make your own with 12 slices of bread dried overnight and toasted 8 minutes at 350⁰ with 1 tbsp. poultry seasoning—had to use this method in Sydney, Australia, while visiting my daughter there)
1 ½ cups chopped onion
1½ cups chopped celery
1 cup chopped carrot
Chopped, boiled giblets, optional (broth can be used in gravy)
1 /2 cup margarine or butter
½ cup broth

1. Place turkey on a large jelly-roll pan. Remove neck and giblets from cavities of turkey. Discard or boil them for the stuffing. Drain juices and pat turkey dry with paper towels. Pour lemon juice in main cavity and over skin. Season inside and out with salt and pepper and sage. Rub herb mixture between the skin and breasts, also.

NOTE: Wash all utensils, work surfaces and hands with hot soapy water after contact with uncooked turkey and juices.

2. Prepare the stuffing: (To roast unstuffed, insert a quartered onion and several celery stalks in cavity)

Cook and stir onion, celery and carrots in margarine in a large skillet over medium heat until tender. Add seasoned bread cubes and broth. Toss to mix. Add more broth if too dry, but make sure mixture is not soggy.

3. Heat oven to 325⁰. Place water on bottom of a large roasting pan. Insert a rack or some kind of turkey lifter.

4. Loosely fill the neck cavity first with stuffing. Use toothpick to hold flap, if necessary. Turn turkey over and fill the body cavity. Tie legs together with kitchen string, band of skin or wire lock. Place turkey, breast side up, in roasting pan. If using a meat thermometer, insert it into innermost part of thigh. Temperature in all areas should be 165⁰ or higher.

5. Cover pan. Roast turkey, basting occasionally with drippings:

8-12 lbs.--2 ¾-3 hours, 12-14 lbs.--3- 3 ½ hours, 14-18 lbs.--3 ¾-4 ½ hours

Stuffed birds take longer than unstuffed. If turkey seems almost done well before serving time, reduce heat to 180⁰ to hold.

Let turkey stand 15 minutes before carving. Remove stuffing to a serving bowl.

TURKEY GRAVY

Pan drippings (collect some into a saucepan during basting) (Remove as much fat as possible with a bulb baster or spoon.)
Turkey, chicken or giblet broth
½ cup flour
Salt and pepper to taste

Pour dripping into a saucepan. Add broth to make 4 cups. In a measuring cup, mix flour and a couple tablespoons of broth until smooth and stir in drippings gradually to blend. Cook and stir until gravy comes to a boil and thickens over medium heat. Cook 3-5 minutes and add salt and pepper. Simmer and adjust consistency with moiré broth if necessary. Add more juices from the turkey platter. Strain out lumps, if necessary. Keep warm until serving time.

SOUR CREAM MASHED POTATOES

2 lbs. potatoes peeled and cut into cubes (about 5 cups to serve 4)
2 tbsp. butter or margarine
1 cup sour cream, regular or soy
Salt and pepper

In a large saucepan, cover potatoes with cold salted water. Bring to a boil and cook 20 minutes or until tender. Drain potatoes and mash them in the pot with a masher. Turn on the heat and whish in the butter and sour cream. Add salt and pepper. Place mashed potatoes in a buttered 2-quart baking dish and bake for 10-15 minutes at 350⁰.

VARIATIONS: Add chopped chives, green onions or roasted garlic.

HOMEMADE CRANBERRY RELISH

1 10 oz. pkg. fresh cranberries
1 cup water
¾ cup sugar
¼ cup fresh orange juice (1/2 of a large orange)
1 strip of orange rind about 3 inches
3 whole cloves or ½ tsp. ground
1 cinnamon stick or 1 tsp. ground cinnamon

Combine all ingredients in a medium saucepan. Bring to a boil, then lower heat and simmer for 20 minutes until cranberries open and mixture thickens. Remove whole cloves and cinnamon stick, if used with a slotted spoon. Place relish in a bowl and refrigerate until ready to use. (Can be made up to 3 days in advance)

ROASTED TURKEY BREAST

1 2 ½ lb. turkey breast half
2 tsp. fresh thyme or 1 tsp. dried
1 tsp. lemon rind, grated
¼ tsp. ground pepper
1/8 tsp. salt
2 cloves garlic, minced

Preheat oven to 400⁰. Combine all ingredients, except turkey, in a small bowl. Loosen skin from turkey and rub on mixture. Press skin down. Place breast half, skin side up on a broiler pan coated with cooking spray. Insert meat thermometer in thickest part of breast, but don't touch the bone. Bake at 400⁰ for 1½ hours or until thermometer reads 180⁰. Let stand 10 minutes. Remove skin, if desired. Cut breast into thin slices.

LEFTOVER TURKEY AND RICE

2 tbsp. margarine or oil
1 cup chopped celery
1 small onion, chopped
1 cup cooked turkey, cubed
1 cup turkey gravy, leftover or from a mix
2 tbsp. flour
1 tsp. salt and pepper to taste
1 ½ cups water or broth
Hot cooked rice

Melt margarine or heat oil in a large saucepan. Add celery and onion. Cook 5 minutes until tender, stirring now and then. Stir in turkey. In a bowl mix gravy, flour, salt and pepper. Add to turkey mixture. Bring to a boil, reduce heat and simmer, uncovered for about 5 minutes. Serve over rice. (serves 4)

SWEET POTATO BAKE

2 ½ lbs. sweet potatoes or 40 oz can sweet potatoes, drained
3 tbsp. butter or margarine
¼ cup pure maple syrup
1 tbsp. brown sugar
1/3 cup pecan halves, chopped
1 ½ cups miniature marshmallows

Grease an 8" square baking dish. Place sweet potatoes in a saucepan with water to cover. Heat to boiling, reduce heat, cover and simmer about 30 minutes until tender.

Drain and cool slightly. Peel and cut into large pieces. Place in baking dish.

In a small saucepan, melt butter or margarine. Stir in syrup and sugar. Cook over low heat while stirring 3-5 minutes. Sprinkle nuts over potatoes and top with syrup mixture. Bake in preheated oven of 350⁰ for 25 minutes. Sprinkle on marshmallows and bake 5-7 minutes until marshmallows are browned.

SWEET POTATO FRIES

Sweet potatoes, as many as needed for serving
Cooking spray
Olive oil
Salt and pepper

Coat a baking sheet with cooking spray. Wash potatoes and cut into sticks. Toss in a bowl with olive oil until lightly coated. Spread out on the baking sheet and season with salt and pepper. Bake at 375⁰ for 40 minutes until soft and lightly browned. Turn halfway through baking.

SWEET POTATO SOUFFLE

3 lbs. sweet potatoes, cubed
1 tsp. salt
1 ½ cups softened butter or margarine
6 large eggs
½ cup flour
3 cups sugar
¼ tsp. cinnamon
1/8 tsp. nutmeg

Boil potatoes with salt until tender. Drain and cool. Place in a blender with other ingredients and process until smooth. Pour into a baking dish. Bake 1 hour or until lightly browned.

SWEET POTATO PIE

2 cups cooked mashed sweet potatoes
1 cup milk, regular or almond
2 eggs
½ cup sugar
1 tbsp. butter or margarine
1 tsp. salt
1 tsp. grated lemon rind

Combine all together and pour into an unbaked 9' pie shell. Bake at 425⁰ for 15 minutes and at 350⁰ until filling is firm and set, about 35 minutes.

PUMPKIN PIE WITH SOY MILK

1 9" pastry shell

¾ cup sugar

1 ¼ tsp. cinnamon

1/ 4 tsp. ginger

1/8 tsp. each nutmeg and cloves

½ tsp. salt

1 can of pumpkin (15 oz.)

1¼ cups soy milk

2 large eggs

Mix sugar and spices in a large bowl. Add pumpkin, milk and eggs. Blend well. Pour all into unbaked pastry crust. Set pie on bottom rack of a 425⁰ oven. Bake 15 minutes and then reduce heat to 350⁰. Bake about 45 minutes longer until center of pie is set. Cool at least 2 hours before serving.

MARZIPAN-TOPPED GLUTEN-FREE CUPCAKES

SEPHARDIC FEST FOR 40TH BIRTHDAY OF MY DAUGHTER, DEVORAH HELFAND, IN LA 2014

AWARD

ABOUT THE AUTHOR

Rachel Almeleh was born in Seattle, Washington to Jewish immigrants from the Isle of Rhodes, which is now Greek, but was Italian at the time of her parent's immigration. Her parents were Sephardic, descendants of Jews exiled from Spain ("Sepharad" in Hebrew), during the Spanish Inquisition of 1492. Their first language was Ladino, a 15th century Spanish which became its own language or dialect with words adopted from many Mediterranean countries and those of the then Ottoman Empire.

At age 12, Rachel lost her mother, who was ill ever since giving birth to the author. The family, including her older sister, Esther, moved to south Seattle where a new Sephardic synagogue was being built. Rachel graduated high school from Rainier Beach and became the first in her family to attend college. She was inspired in middle school to become a Spanish teacher and that she did after graduating from the University of Washington in 1967.

Her first teaching job was at Cleveland High School in the Seattle School District, where she taught Spanish and her minor, French. Her French was not good enough to teach advanced classes, so she spent a summer quarter studying nothing but French. Whatever Rachel does, she likes to do it well. She is very goal-oriented. After marriage and the birth of her first child, a home was purchased in Federal Way and 14 years of teaching ensued at Foster High School in Tukwila, WA.

During these years, Rachel tried to perfect her cooking skills with Sephardic food to pass on the traditions of her family. As well as adopting language from different countries, Sephardics also adopted their cuisine: a little Turkish, a little Italian, a little Israeli, a lot of Greek, etc. Rachel would visit her aunties and watch them cook and write down recipes with a few secrets here and there. Her dream of selling "borecas" began to brew.

After marriage in 1970 and two children later, Rachel went back to school at the UW, six summers, to get her Master's, a goal to be able to teach community college. Her thesis about how to teach foreign languages was her first published work. In 1990, after 20 years of marriage, Rachel divorced. While living in Federal Way, WA, she hatched her hobby business, Rachel's Sephardic Delicacies. Cooking Sephardic food was a passion to be shared, to nurture all those she loved and cared about and all those who loved Sephardic food.

Index

CPSIA information can be obtained
at www.ICGtesting.com
Printed in the USA
FSOW03n1138270815
10360FS